Bevon

The Omega Bell

A Firefighter's Last Alarm

Foreword by Hal Bruno

Note: Names of some people throughout this book have been changed.

ISBN: 0-87148-071-9

Printed by *Derek Press*
Cleveland, Tennessee 37311

Frontispiece

Paul Harold Smith

March 3, 1967 – December 25, 1989

Born of Love Died with Honor

The Omega Bell

A Firefighter's Last Alarm

FOREWORD

"The risks are plain . . . when a man becomes a fireman, his act of bravery already has been accomplished."

Those words were spoken a century ago by Edward F. Croker, a legendary chief of the Fire Department of New York. They are just as true today and apply to every man and woman who takes the oath to be a firefighter. An average of 100 firefighters die in the line of duty every year and thousands more are injured in America's big cities, suburbs and small towns, both paid and volunteer fire departments.

Whenever a firefighter dies in the line of duty, there must be an investigation to determine what went wrong—what new lessons should be learned, what old lessons were unheeded and need to be reemphasized. We can never be complacent and must never accept a line-of-duty death as inevitable. Steps have to be taken to prevent it from happening again, even though we know that the work is inherently dangerous and each year more names will be added to the National Fallen Firefighters Memorial in Emmitsburg, Maryland—site of the National Fire Academy.

Along with the investigation, we must honor the memory of our fallen firefighters and do all that we can to support their families in their time of need. They too must perform their own act of bravery by rebuilding their lives and going forward to the future, as the firefighters they lost would want and expect them to do. It is the mission of the National Fallen Firefighters Foundation to help them make that long and difficult journey.

That is where I came to know the Reverend Bevon Smith, a Church of God minister who serves as one of the Foundation's chaplains. He and his family became involved after his son, Paul, a Greenville, Mississippi, firefighter was fatally injured while fighting an apartment building fire in 1989. As Bevon explains in this book, everything that could go wrong went wrong—in both the fire and its tragic aftermath. In the years since, they have been committed to counseling the families of fallen firefighters to help them avoid the mistakes that were made when they went through their ordeal. Bevon has also been part of the Foundation's team that trains chaplains and senior fire officers on how to deal with a line-of-duty death when it occurs in their department.

On September 11, 2001, the entire world learned about heroism when 347 firefighters were killed in the terrorist attack on New York's World Trade Center. On a massive scale, never seen before, it showed the spirit of the fire-rescue services and what firefighters do every day as they risk their lives to save others. On a small scale, it's what Paul Smith was doing when he entered that burning building in Greenville, Mississippi, on December 3, 1989.

Inevitably, it raises the question of *why* they do it. The answer is that each does it for his own reasons—the challenge it presents, a quest for excitement, pride in doing a tough, dirty and dangerous job that most people are unable or unwilling to do. Whatever the reason, they do it with enthusiasm and total commitment and never think of themselves as being heroes, though their actions often are heroic. They are intensely loyal to their company and the comrades they serve with, bonding together like a family. They enjoy the laughter and horseplay of firehouse life while waiting for that jolt of adrenaline a firefighter experiences every time the alarm bell rings. For them, nothing equals the satisfaction of being part of the fire-rescue team and using their strength and skill to knock down a raging fire, save a person trapped in a burning building, control a hazardous material leak, or give emergency medical care to a person injured in an accident or suffering from a painful illness.

As Bevon describes his son, it is clear that Paul had the enthusiasm and commitment to be a firefighter. It took his life, but it is the life he chose to live. In fact, it is difficult to imagine Paul Smith following any other path. This is the story of one young firefighter and his family, the sacrifice they made, the pain they endured, and the long, slow healing process. The passage of time does not dim memories or close wounds, but as Bevon and his family demonstrate, it can teach you how to live with the loss you suffered—if you have faith and the will to learn.

—Hal Bruno,
Chairman National Fallen Firefighters Foundation
ABC News Political Director (Retired)

To my wife, Frances,

my children, Dawn, Joey, and Stevie,

who shared with me as no others could,

the joy of Paul's life and the heartbreak of his death.

CONTENTS

PREFACE

The Omega Bell: A Firefighter's Last Alarm is a gripping personal account of a father's experience in having to deal with the death of his son. Dealing with the loss of a loved one is a difficult task in and of itself, but adding to this the tragic circumstances of Paul Smith's death—while battling a fire—makes this story especially poignant. The agonizing details that Bevon Smith shares about his personal struggles will strike a chord with others who have experienced the trauma of losing a loved one in death.

The fact that death is a part of the human experience is little consolation when one stands before a casket or at an open grave site. Words often mean very little to those experiencing the sudden pain of grief and loss, but actions of love and support are vividly remembered long after the funeral service.

The story of Paul Smith is very touching and emotionally heartrending. It vividly captures the gamut of emotional responses a person experiences in dealing with a tragic death. Bevon Smith is to be commended for his honest and forthright description of the questions that remain unanswered, the guilt of words not spoken or actions not taken, and the lingering heartache that gnaws at one's efforts to resume a "normal" life.

I recommend this book to anyone struggling with the death of a loved one as well as to those who minister to individuals experiencing tragedy. Knowing that we are not alone in the thoughts we think, or the pain we feel, or the struggles we experience can be of great comfort.

R. Lamar Vest, D.Litt
Administrative Bishop, Church of God
Cleveland, Tennessee

May 2004

ACKNOWLEDGMENTS

I wish to acknowledge the assistance of Homer G. Rhea, L.H.D. whose patience, encouragement, and professional guidance in this endeavor have been invaluable.

Others have also been a very valuable source of help to me throughout this whole ordeal:

1. **The National Fallen Firefighters Foundation** for giving me the opportunity to share a snapshot of Paul's life around the nation.

2. **The Creve Coeur, Missouri, Fire Department** who considered Paul as a brother.

3. **The Trinity Heights Church of God** who graciously allows us to share our story and our time with so many.

—Bevon Joe Smith

INTRODUCTION

I knew Bevon and Frances Smith quite a while before Paul was born. Both were campers and workers in youth camp when I served as state youth director for the Church of God in Mississippi. I actually think they fell in love during those camps, and a few years later I had the privilege of returning to Mississippi to perform their wedding ceremony. When Paul graced their home with his presence, they graced my life by naming him after me. From that day forward, Paul Smith had a special place in my heart. On many occasions, I spent time in the Smith home and, although I was usually there on church business, the enjoyment of Paul and his siblings was always a highlight of my visit.

Paul's love for gospel music began to take form early in his life. He developed rapidly into an excellent musician and never seemed to consider using his talents for anything but the church. He became a partner with his preacher dad, his mom, his brothers and sister who made up one of the best singing and ministry families the Church has ever produced. I have never met a young man who had a greater love and respect for his dad than Paul. When possible, he wanted to be with him. If, as a young person, he ever went through a period of rebellion against his parents or his church, it never became evident.

When word first came to me that Bevon Smith would like for me to write this introduction, my first thought was, *he was too young to write a book about him*. But when I started thinking seriously about his personality and his life, I quickly changed my mind.

Even though Paul is no longer with us, his

influence lives on. For example, his influence as a firefighter has opened up opportunities for his dad to tell his story from Miami to San Francisco. His influence as a Christian has opened the Memorial Medical Clinic in Madras, India. Thousands of poor children are medically treated each year at this clinic. The gospel message of love and compassion is told to the parents who bring their children for help. This has resulted in hundreds of them being converted to Christ.

As years go, Paul lived a relatively short life. Yet, he poured a lot of living into those few short years. I have read about another man—Jesus—whose story is told in the Bible. He lived a short life as we count years, months, weeks, hours, minutes and seconds. Where His living really shows up is in His loving, caring, forgiving, healing, and helping. How much we live is truly more important than how long we live. The same was true with Paul. He poured his love and care into a few short years. Bevon has captured the essence of Paul's short life, presenting it for the reader with great love and passion.

—Paul F. Henson

Chapter 1

A Flight Too Soon!

His hand was placed gently on the beautifully crafted natural oak casket, now resting on the lowering device over an open grave. Flowers, greenery, and artificial grass had been placed around the grave to give a soft and gentle appearance to what was a very hard, cruel, and painful experience. Yet as beautiful as they made it, it did not soften the devastating pain nor dull the harshness of the moment.

Beneath the colorful flowers and imitation grass awaited an ugly dark hole in a frozen ground. Like a monster with its mouth open wide, it waited to receive the precious young body that would soon be lowered into its belly.

The sky was gray on that cold December day, and the winds came sweeping across that little hilltop cemetery with a biting chill. He spoke softly as he looked into our faces, "I know how you are hurting, and I know the pain you are feeling," he said. He then told the story of a most unusual painting found in the Louvre in Paris. Depicted was a group of caterpillars marching in prossession carrying an old empty cocoon on their shoulders. Their heartbreak and extravagant crying are signs of great mourning. They are heartbroken and crying profusely because the caterpillar that once lived inside the cocoon is now gone. Yet as they marched, right above their heads floated a beautiful, colorful butterfly, fluttering about in the soft breeze. "It's very much like that with us today," he said, "We mourn as we place this body in the grave, but even now Paul is high above our heads in a brand new life." The Reverend Paul F. Henson, a minister that I hold in highest esteem, and a long-time friend of our family, spoke these words at the committal service of our son Paul. He proceeded to read Scripture and pray in the traditional manner.

There we were sitting under the canvas canopy, which shielded us from the misting rain falling around us. It was as if the heavens felt our sorrow and were weeping with us on that day. As we sat there, a thousand questions passed through my mind. *This is not supposed to be this way,* I thought. Parents are not supposed to bury their children. Children should bury their parents, that is the natural order of life. But today that order is violated; today we are burying our son. He was only 22 years of age, so talented, so good, so caring, so loving, so full of life, and yet dead at this young age when most of his life was still before him. He had barely stepped onto the stage of adulthood when he was suddenly cut down. *How fair is this?* I thought. I sat there fighting back tears that struggled to burst free and flow as a river.

Suddenly the air was filled with the beautiful sounds of a trombone solo of *Amazing Grace* played by David Redden, one of Paul's musician friends who stood concealed just at the edge of the cemetery. At our request, *Amazing Grace* was played rather than the traditional Taps. As he played, all the people joined in, singing along with the music. After the song came the handshakes and sympathetic expressions of the officiating clergy. Then we were directed to move from the grave site for a period of time and return after the grave closing was completed.

I sat there looking at the casket that contained the body of my precious son; I would never see him again in this life. As someone nudged me to move from under the canopy, I thought I just couldn't move away. Each step I took was harder and harder; he was there behind me, and I was walking away. Somewhere between the grave and the cemetery gates, I turned around and approached the funeral director. "Open the casket and let me see him one more time," I pleaded. With a look of dismay on his face, he reluctantly agreed to open the casket at the grave and let me see Paul again. I took a deep breath as I walked beside the now open casket and looked at my son for the last time. It did not look like him at all. Paul was a handsome young man with such clear skin, beautiful dark black hair and the most beautiful teeth and smile. His face had been so badly burned and disfigured by the fire until he looked nothing like himself. The morticians had tried to restore his facial features to a natural appearance, but try as they had, it was to no avail. Yet, beneath all the wax, the makeup, and the rough, it was Paul. It was my son lying there in that casket. It was a very emotional experience for me. I said my good-bye, turned and slowly walked away.

Through the years, I have preached many funerals of young people. The last funeral I conducted in St. Louis, Missouri, before our move back to Mississippi, was of a 17-year-old high school senior. We had been in Greenville, Mississippi, hardly three months before I preached the funeral of another high school senior. Both young men were killed in automobile accidents.

Regardless of the funerals I had preached it was always a son or a daughter, it was never my son. It was always *their* son or *their* daughter; it was always *someone else's* son, it was never my son. As I stood in the cemetery that day, it was no longer *a* son, no longer *their* son, it was now my son! There, that day, I realized that I had not really understood what the parents of those young people had gone through. I thought I knew; I thought I understood; but I was wrong; I was so wrong. Now that it was my son, it made a world of difference. This was the end of a beautiful life on earth for Paul. It was the beginning of a long, hard, and difficult journey for my family and me.

Chapter 2

The Story Begins

This story actually began nearly 23 years before, March 3, 1967, to be exact. I remember so clearly the event, and for me it truly was an event. I was a young, inexperienced husband and pastor of a small church in a southern city. My wife had been admitted to the local hospital for the birth of our first child. My family was there, friends came in, and there was our ever faithful and caring family physician of many years, Dr. Joe Powell.

I tried hard to appear calm and relaxed, but I was almost a basket case. The hours passed slowly as we waited with excitement for the grand event to occur. At some point, I was summoned to my wife's room where she was already in hard labor. I could not handle this very well, so I thought of an excuse to leave as soon as I could. I walked into the hallway and paced from one end of the hallway to the other for what seem to be forever.

The waiting was finally over and they took my wife to the delivery room. They rolled her past us on a Gurney, and I shall always remember how beautiful she looked. As she passed by me, I thought of the first time I saw her. It was at a church youth camp in June 1962. I had been invited as the speaker for the youth meeting at the Kittiewake Baptist Campground on the Mississippi Gulf Coast. I had not noticed her in the nightly services. One night after the lights were out, I took a walk in the night air. Passing by the dining hall, I saw a group of young people who were helping with a special project. I went inside, and there she was in that group of young people. I remember how beautiful she looked that night. She stood out from the others. And from that moment forward, I could not get her out of my mind. I also remembered how lovely she looked as she walked down the aisle on the arm of her father on our wedding day. But never before had she looked as beautiful as she did on that day.

I kissed her and watched as she disappeared through the heavy swinging doors. I stood there wondering about what went on in there anyway, but I did not want to go back there to find out. I turned and smiled at those gathered to wait with us, then I began to walk again.

This was in the days before it was possible to know the sex of a baby before birth, and I wondered if it would be a boy or a girl. Would it be normal? What if something happened to her or the baby? I guess I was really hoping for a boy, but I knew that I would be just as happy if it were a girl. Dr. Powell came to me and informed me that he thought he should give my wife an epidural because she had a very low tolerance of pain. I agreed with him, as if I knew what he was talking about.

I do not recall the exact time before a nurse came to the door and told me that I had a big boy back there. I joyfully exclaimed to my waiting family, "A boy!" Later, another nurse brought him out to us wrapped in his blue receiving blanket. I took my first look at him and how wonderful he looked. His head covered with dark black hair, his big beautiful eyes open wide, and his little hand shaped into a tiny fist. How happy and proud I was, I wanted to cry. Never before in all my life had I experienced anything quite like that moment. There is really no way to describe the feeling when a man is permitted to take his first steps into that mystical land of fatherhood. There was a new life, a part of me, so pretty and so innocent, what a joy; I was now a father! What a privilege!

They placed the baby in the nursery, which was small with a very small window from the hallway. I stood at that tiny window and gazed upon my newborn son for hours. Even then I had dreams of what he might become in life. I envisioned great and happy days ahead for him. However, they were just that, dreams. Happiness somehow eluded Paul for most of his short life.

The hospital experience was soon over, and we brought our boy home. Our first home was really a manufactured home. It was nice and comfortable, but limited in many things that a regular constructed home provides. But it was our home, and we were happy with our little family together. While living in that home, we celebrated Paul's first birthday, with my wife baking his first birthday cake.

Our family would soon grow again with the birth of our second child, a daughter, whom we named Dawn. Very rapidly our humble abode was getting a bit crowded, and we needed extra room. I was able to purchase a house in the Ponderosa Subdivision of Southwest Picayune, Mississippi, and we joyfully moved into our lovely three-bedroom brick home.

At that time I was employed by Boeing Aerospace, working at the NASA Computer Center in Slidell, Louisiana. Besides working with Boeing, I was the pastor of a small, but growing church in Picayune. I was making a good salary with Boeing plus the income from the church. We were doing nicely at that time in our lives. We lived in a nice new house, we had two cars and a boat, and we were comfortable.

It was during our time in Picayune that Paul experienced his first admission to a hospital. He suffered a stomach disorder that required overnight treatment in the hospital. I stayed with him that night and entertained him because there was no television in the room.

I enjoyed my job with Boeing. It was interesting, but challenging, and I worked with a good group of people. The church was growing with new people almost every month. But when I should have been the most content, something happened to me. I began to feel very restless. I became troubled in my spirit and I had a strong desire to be in ministry full time, something I had never been able to do.

The church had experienced growth, but they did not think they were strong enough financially to support a full-time pastor. I would have continued as the pastor if the church had supported me. They had convinced themselves they could not provide the financial support I needed; and neither did they think I would leave my good job with Boeing. I felt that this left me only one option, to resign the church and enter another field of ministry. I also had to make a decision about whether or not to leave my secular job and the security it afforded us, which would mean a drastic change in our lifestyle. I wrestled with this for some time and spent much time in prayer before I made my final decision.

Our denomination conducted a state convention in June of each year. All ministers were expected to attend the entire week of activities. Because of my job, I would be able to attend only a couple of the night services. But I felt impressed to take a week off from work and attend the entire convention. While there, a member of the State Evangelism Board came to me and asked me to consider becoming the state evangelist. Their offer was not much financially—one hundred dollars a month, plus any offerings received in the revival meetings I led.

I called my wife at home in Picayune and talked with her about it. I know she was shocked to hear that I was even considering this offer. As always, she gave her total support to me, trusting the direction that I believed the Lord wanted for our lives. This time she knew it would be hard, but if God wanted us to do it, she believed we would make it.

I returned to work and completed the remainder of the month of June. Giving my resignation was difficult. My supervisor talked with me privately in his office for a long time trying to persuade me to reconsider my decision. He made a tempting promise to me if I would stay, but I felt strongly that I had to go into full-time ministry. I worked my final day for Boeing on July 2, 1970.

We arranged to live with my wife's mother who lived alone in a rather large house in Starkville. Frances took Dawn and went to Starkville that same day (July 2, 1970). Paul and I brought some furniture and our clothing in a U-Haul trailer the next day. I remember that trip so vividly. We finished loading the largest trailer U-Haul had, ate breakfast, and set out as early as we could for Starkville. Paul was about four years old and felt as big as his daddy that day. He was so happy that we were going to live with Grandma. To this day, there are places along I-59 south of Meridian, Mississippi, where I get a lump in my throat when I travel past them. I recall something we did or something we said as we traveled together on that trip, it was a special time together.

Arriving in Starkville, I had a difficult time parking the extra long tandem-wheel trailer in the driveway. It was so large and so packed that it pushed the rear of my new 1969 Plymouth VIP almost to the ground. But we had made it there safely, and now we would begin a new chapter in our lives.

It was a blessing for us to be able to live with Mrs. Ruth Griffin; Frances' mother. Living with her, we did not have to pay rent or utilities, and she was a good cook also.

My plan was to preach revivals in churches that invited me and depend entirely upon their freewill offerings to support my family. It was going to be a real test of management skills, discipline, and faith. The financial problem involved more than the loss of a steady income, when I left Boeing I lost the medical insurance for my family and the life insurance on myself. Our faith was really put to the test, and we wondered just how we would survive. But we were committed to giving it our best effort and depending on the Lord to help us.

I had scheduled some revivals during the convention week in Jackson. My first revival was conducted in Columbus the first week in July 1970. The pastor and his wife, Hulon and Margie Evans, encouraged us and helped us feel that we had made the correct decision.

I was gone most of the time and came home as often as the revival schedules permitted. Often after I preached, I would drive across the state to be with my family for just a few hours and then return to the same church for the service the following night. I couldn't miss a revival service because that meant losing an offering, and I was hardly making it financially. So I pushed myself. I wanted to be with my family, but I had to also be on the job preaching. I burned the candle at both ends, but so what . . . I was young and I could do it.

My wife's parents had been in the grocery business for many years in Starkville. Their business had recently been sold to a retired school administrator. One morning he came to Mrs. Griffin's home and wanted to know if she would be willing to take over the store and operate it. She told him that she was not interested in the store but her daughter and son-in-law might be.

She arranged for us to meet with him and discuss the proposal. It became immediately apparent that he was not cut out for the grocery store business. He wanted out as badly as anybody I've ever seen. He wanted out so badly, he was almost crying. He made us an offer that was unheard of. He said, "You just walk in, and I'll just walk out. We won't even take inventory; you don't have to buy my stock. You operate the store for six months or a year, then should you want out, just walk out, and I'll walk back in." I had never heard of anything like that. I wouldn't even have to pay rent until we had been in operation for a month. I thought this must surely be from the Lord. I did not have the money to buy his inventory or pay a lease on the facilities, but I could do what he was offering. We thought it over for a day or two and prayed about it. We all three agreed that this was the thing we should do.

Frances and Mrs. Griffin operated the store, and when I was home between revivals, I would help. Mrs. Griffin had many years' experience and had been very successful in the grocery business. Frances was raised in that very same store, and she knew the business inside out.

All the old customers were so happy to see Mrs. Griffin back in the store that business picked up in a very short time and was booming just like old times. The store gave us the extra income we needed to meet our expenses at the time.

Not being able to take my family with me when I conducted revivals was very difficult for me. However, there were times when I would take Paul with me. Even though he was a little kid—four to five years old—he was always easy to care for, and absolutely no trouble at all. He was polite, had good manners, and everyone enjoyed having him around.

You should have seen the look on some of the pastors' faces when I first arrived to spend a week at their church with my little boy. They just knew that meant trouble for them, but it never did. During each service as I preached, Paul would sit on the front pew of the church like a little man. He never moved or made a sound the entire service. Most of the people could not believe how good he was. Many of the pastors would tell me at the close of a revival, "Come back again, and be sure to bring little Paul with you."

I was conducting a revival in Cleveland, Mississippi, when I received a call from a family in my hometown. A man that I had known all my life was very sick and not expected to live. He told his family that he had to talk with me before he died. They wanted me to come to the hospital and talk with him. I told them that I was in a revival and could not miss a service. I explained that it would be very difficult for me to make the trip, but they pleaded with me to come.

I had visited this man and invited him to church many times when I pastored in his community a few years before. I never did get him to attend church, but he was always kind and friendly toward me. He must have respected me more than I knew by summoning me to his dying bed. I wondered, *What could he want to talk with me about?*

It was very difficult for me to drive to Poplarville and back to Cleveland in such short time, but I made the decision to go. So after service that night, I put Paul in the car and the two of us started out on a drive that took several hours. Paul talked for a while then he got sleepy. When he got sleepy enough, he crawled into my lap and rode in my lap the rest of the way to my parents' home in Poplarville.

I went to the hospital the next morning and talked with the man and learned what was troubling him. He was wrestling with something from his past that he felt prevented him from getting his life right with the Lord. I listened as he spoke through the plastic walls of an oxygen tent placed over his bed. I talked to him at length, then I gave him scriptures to assure him that he could find peace with the Lord. After our talk, he appeared to clear his mind and conscience of the guilt he felt. He then prayed the sinner's prayer.

Paul and I got into our automobile and drove back to Cleveland for the next revival service. Not only was Paul not a problem for me during the entire trip, but he also kept me company. Those really were special times for me.

Chapter 3

He Gave Us a Song

Very early in his life Paul developed a strong interest in music. He received his first set of drums when he was five years old and immediately began to show great musical promise. He taught himself to play drums by playing along with Christian recording artists such as Sammy Hall, The Fowlers, and others. He would amaze his friends and family members with his playing. Even at a young age it was obvious that he possessed a special talent for music. Apparently, some people are born with an innate ability that enables them to develop skills in music far beyond the average level of achievement. This gift is often referred to as natural talent. Paul, it seems, was one of those special people. In addition to his natural talent, he practiced very hard to develop his musical skills. He set very high goals for himself and was never satisfied with anything less than the best he could become.

I had accepted the call to pastor a church in Charleston, Mississippi, before Paul began his school years. There was a young man in that church who was a very talented singer and electric bass guitar player. His family was involved in singing gospel music. They traveled across the state singing in revivals, homecomings, and other special events. Even though he was several years older than Paul, Bobby took a special interest in Paul and helped him develop his skills on the drums and began teaching him to play the bass guitar. The bass guitar became one of Paul's favorite instruments, and it was one he would master to perfection in the years ahead.

Paul became the drummer for the Rowe Family and traveled with them across the state. While traveling with the Rowe Family, he met Cheryl Pruitt who later became the 1980 Miss America. After her crowning, Paul enjoyed telling his friends that he knew Miss America and she had kissed him. This was true, even though Paul was only eight years old at the time.

While living in Charleston, we purchased a piano and Paul began piano lessons. He learned quickly. But Paul's ability to play by ear became a problem for him. He wanted to go ahead and play the music without practicing. His music teacher was not too happy when he did that.

After living in Charleston almost six years, we moved to Jackson, Mississippi, where we became friends with the Arrinder Family. They were great musicians, and the father, Lonnie, played the steel guitar. Lonnie gave Paul a few lessons on the steel, and he learned rapidly. We bought him a single neck BMI pedal steel guitar, and he immediately began to play a number of tunes. He continued playing the other instruments also. It was at that time he began to teach his younger brother Joey to play the drums.

While we lived in Jackson, Paul began taking piano lessons from Brenda O'Neal, a pastor's wife, who was an extremely accomplished pianist herself. She quickly recognized Paul's natural ability with the piano, but she also encouraged him to continue his music lessons, which he did. He loved his music and would practice for hours at a time.

Sometimes his practice would be a real test of patience and nerves for the rest of the family.

Thankfully, his drums were set up in the sanctuary of our church so he could play all he wanted without driving the family insane.

After three years in Jackson, we moved to St. Louis, Missouri, to pastor the Webster Groves Church of God. While in St. Louis, Paul was able to take steel guitar lessons from Pat Hiller and Dewitt Scott, two very popular instructors. He advanced so quickly with the steelguitar that we bought him a double neck "Sho Bud" steel that had ten pedals and four knee levers. To be an accomplished player of this instrument requires great skill. He was displaying this skill at age twelve.

Paul always enjoyed attending the National Steel Guitar Conventions, which were held in St. Louis annually. I would go with him when my schedule permitted. Sometimes, I was not always able to stay at the convention with him, and naturally I did not feel comfortable leaving him alone. Once, he wanted to stay so badly until Jimmy Day, one of Nashville's greatest steel players, felt sorry for him and agreed to watch over him in my absence. During one of the conventions, a very famous Nashville musician told me that Paul had the talent to become a really great steel guitar player. He became a good friend with musicians Buddy Emmons and Jimmy Day. Both encouraged him to perfect his skills with the steel.

Paul played in our Webster Groves church each Sunday. It was during this time that Paul, Dawn, and Joey began to sing and play together in our local church. Soon they were receiving invitations to sing in revivals and state meetings throughout Missouri. It was always a great joy for me to have them travel with me and sing when I preached revival meetings. They always added so much to the services. When other singers came to our church, they always wanted Paul to play with them. It amazed me that he could play right along with them regardless of who the singers were, or their style of music.

There was a man in St. Louis County with a country music band who wanted Paul to play the steel guitar in his band. After we learned that he sometimes played in nightclubs, we declined his offer. He just could not understand why we would not allow a talented young man like Paul to play in his band. We never told him that Paul did not want to play in his band.

St. Louis was our home for almost nine years. By this time, Paul and Dawn had graduated from high school and Dawn was attending Lee College in Cleveland, Tennessee. We moved back to Mississippi to pastor the New Life Church of God in Greenville. This church had a very good music program with some very talented musicians and singers. Jewell Johnson served as church pianist and was one of the finest that I have heard. She and her family also formed a gospel singing group that traveled almost every week to fill engagements.

Once again Paul became a vital part of the great music program of that church. He had developed his talents as a singer as well as a musician. The congregation there always enjoyed his special songs. There was something different about his singing that touched many people very deeply. He had a beautiful voice, but even though it was not the most beautiful voice in the world, there was an anointing on him that would deeply touch his audience. Paul enjoyed teaming with other singers and musicians in what he called "jamming." Some of those who joined with him in such music sessions were: The Porter Family of

Forrest City, Arkansas; Lemuel Miller of Wildwood, Florida; The Johnson Family and Calvin Barksdale of Greenville, Mississippi; and Terry and Teresa Baker of Wichita, Kansas, to name a few. His versatility was truly remarkable. Several months before his accident, I encouraged Paul to make a professional recording of some of the songs he sang, which was a task he was never able to accomplish.

New Harvest, a musical group from Lee College, visited our church for special services. They had recently lost their regular bass guitar player and were without one at the time of their arrival. Paul played the bass for them over the weekend, and before they left town, they had invited Paul to join their group and move to Cleveland, Tennessee. We hated to see him leave us, but we were happy that he had an opportunity to advance his music ministry as a member of this group. Paul had been working with the Greenville Fire Department prior to this occasion. When he resigned his job with the fire department, Chief Williamson told him that if he ever wanted his old job back, that it would be waiting for him.

He lived in Cleveland and shared an apartment with a couple of other young men who were members of the group. During that time he traveled with Danny Murray, Judy Jacobs and New Harvest across the nation playing and singing. They traveled in a specially equipped Silver Eagle bus that he enjoyed. After a short time, Danny began to use him as an assistant driver. He remained with the group for several months. That was a special time in his life. He loved each member in the group and considered it an honor to be associated with them. As time passed, Paul made the decision to return to his job with the Greenville Fire Department. As much as he loved music and enjoyed being a member of New Harvest, the desire to be a firefighter continued within him.

Returning home, Paul again involved himself in our church music program. I asked him to consider directing our cantata for Easter that year. He was reluctant at first, but after praying about it, and thinking about it, he accepted the challenge. His time was limited because of his hours with the fire department. However, he devoted himself to making it the best it could be. He was disappointed that a few of the singers in the church chose not to participate. He was strongly depending on them for solo parts in the cantata, and he could not understand why they refused. Nevertheless, he did not give up and quit.

He recruited new members for the choir, and worked very hard with some who had never had a featured solo part before. They were nervous and unsure of themselves as soloists, but Paul worked one-on-one with them, he encouraged them, and made them feel good about their ability. To the surprise of many people, each of them really did a very good job with their parts. He worked very hard to secure needed props and choir risers, as well as promoting the presentation. There was a great deal of logistics involved with the production, but he wanted to make it a success, so he pushed himself far beyond what was expected. During this time, I was able to assist him with many of the physical chores, which proved to be a very special time for the two of us.

The choir gave their performance on Easter Sunday, March 26, 1989. It was a very moving and powerful presentation. For many years our churches have presented musical specials, especially for Easter and Christmas. They are beautiful, but it has been my experience that they often become performances rather than worship. I can truly say that cantata was completely different than most. The Spirit of the Lord was present from the very beginning. Every song touched the hearts of the congregation. When Paul sang his solo parts, people were spellbound. At the close of the cantata, nine adults came forward and professed their acceptance of Jesus Christ. I had never witnessed anything like that in my entire ministry. It was such a powerful presentation that people talked about it for years afterward.

After the beautiful and inspiring musical presented in the sanctuary Easter Sunday morning, we moved to the large church gymnasium for the evening service. That particular service was referred to as "The Lord's Table." A huge table was set up in the shape of a cross. The table was set with loaves of unleavened bread, clusters of grapes, lilies, candles, and greenery. A place was set at the head of the table with a large chair draped with a robe and a crown of thrones. The entire service was set in candlelight with soft background music. It made for a very impressive experience.

In this beautiful setting, we celebrated Holy Communion. As that service progressed, I suddenly had a very strange and strong impression that something terrible was going to occur. I felt that my family would face some great tragedy before that year ended. This impression weighed so heavily upon me that I called my family together and asked the church to pray a special prayer for us. The six of us stood together before the church as they prayed. After the prayer, the service continued as planned. Call it coincidence, call it divine inspiration, or call it what you will, it really happened to us, and I was reminded of this shortly after Paul's death.

Chapter 4

Our Time in St. Louis

I served as pastor of the North Jackson Church of God for three years, during which time the church experienced good growth in membership and finance. We completed the construction of a new Christian education wing to the church and things were looking very positive. I had settled in for a long-term pastorate in Jackson.

I had served the North Jackson church for three years when things changed abruptly for us. I was in my office on a Sunday morning when I received a phone call from the state superintendent of Missouri. He asked me if I could talk. I said, "Yes." He told me that at that very moment he was in his office praying about a church in St. Louis that was without a pastor. He said he felt the Lord directing him to call me about accepting the Webster Groves Church of God. Webster Groves is a nice bedroom community located in St. Louis County, Missouri.

I was caught completely off guard. I did not know anything about that particular church, and I really had no plans to move from Jackson. He pressed me for an answer that morning, but I just could not give him one. He wanted me to give my resignation to the Jackson church in the morning worship service. That was something else I could not bring myself to do. He proceeded to tell me he had a meeting scheduled that morning with the Webster Groves church for them to vote for a new pastor. He said that he would recommend me to the church. This was quite an honor, but it was all happening too fast, and I was not prepared to make a decision. I needed some time.

I did not resign the North Jackson church that morning as he suggested. I just could not bring myself to do it, I was so unsure about what to do. In fact I did not even say anything to my family about the call until later in the afternoon. When I did tell them, they got all excited about the possibility. "Why didn't you tell us sooner?" they asked. After we discussed it, we each agreed to make it a matter of prayer. As he promised, the superintendent called me back that afternoon. He was a bit surprised when he learned that I had not resigned my church in Jackson.

Several days passed before I made my decision. During that time, I received calls from some of the local leaders in the Missouri church. Each of them had very positive things to say about my becoming their pastor. I also spoke with the state superintendent several times during that period. Being from the South, I was concerned about being accepted by that large Midwestern church. Each time we talked, I was assured that everything would work out just fine.

Several days passed before I called the church board together in Jackson and told them my decision. It was one of the hardest decisions I had ever made. The men in that church had been very good to my family and me. They helped us turn that church around, and they worked very hard to see it grow. One man in particular, Lavon Pilgrim, had been a great supporter and true friend. My children loved him and his family dearly. I could tell that he was hurt by my decision to leave North Jackson. It was hard to leave them, but we believed the Lord was directing our move.

We were under great pressure to get packed and move that long distance. The Webster Groves church wanted us to move as soon as possible, and we understood that. We were struggling with the logistics of moving all our belongings to St. Louis when the Webster Groves church decided to use a professional moving company.

After packing our belongings and watching them loaded into the moving van, we got into our vehicles and started out for our new home in St. Louis. It was December 1978, and we were experiencing one of the most severe ice storms that had ever hit the South. Frances took Dawn and Stevie, who was only 6 months old, in our Ford LTD car. I took Paul and Joey with me in our Plymouth van pulling a U-Haul type trailer. We made it to Memphis and spent the night in a motel there.

We arrived at the church around 6 o'clock that Saturday evening and saw that there were many automobiles in the church parking lot. I thought all those people had come out to welcome their new pastor and his family. But that was not the case. They were there for choir rehearsal for the upcoming Christmas cantata.

There was one man, the Reverend W.E. Dillow, who was waiting for us. That faithful member of the church came out to welcome us. He immediately took us under his wing and helped us get settled. He purchased food for us, and did everything he could to make our first night in St. Louis comfortable. He proved to be one of our truest friends and greatest supporters.

The church was filled on our first Sunday. Everybody came out to meet the new pastor. I soon learned that I followed a man, John Walker, whose shoes would be hard to fill, but I was certainly going to do my best. The state overseer, the Reverend Paul Barker, presented my family to the church during the morning service. I preached my first sermon that morning, but I think many of the people almost needed an interpreter due to my strong Southern accent. But soon they began to understand and love it. I had most of them saying "Y'all" before I left the church. We got through that first Sunday and felt really good about the new church.

The next item on our agenda was to enroll our children in Clark Elementary School in Webster Groves. It was a good school in a very good school system. I expected Joey to be apprehensive about attending a new school, maybe Dawn, but not Paul. However, to my surprise, it was Paul who was most affected by the change in schools. I remember while we were in the principal's office how he tried to fight back his tears of frustration. Once the children were enrolled things went much better, or at least I thought they were better.

Paul was in the sixth grade—an age when children can be cruel and hurtful to other children and never realize what they are doing. We soon found that Paul began to dislike school; in fact, we saw a change in him which concerned us. We learned that some of the other boys in his class called him names like "Mississippi hillbilly" and "Pig farmer." Paul took this insult very personally, and it hurt him deeply. Because Clark Elementary went through only the sixth grade, Paul had only a half year there. We encouraged him, and prayed for him and he finished that year successfully.

He attended Hixon Junior High his next two years. We thought it would be better for him at Hixon than it was at Clark. Paul never said much about school, he just went about his routine without complaining. At this time, he became more involved in his music. Perhaps his music became an escape from disappointments and hurts. He spent many, many hours practicing piano, steel guitar, and the bass guitar.

All this time I thought everything was going well at school until one day I passed by his school as I made a trip into the city. It happened to be during a break period. I saw the campus was covered with school kids at play: some running, some playing softball, others sitting together talking. I found my eyes fixed on the schoolyard for no apparent reason, and as I scanned the school activity area, my eyes fell on one kid who was all by himself and far away from all the others. He was walking back and forth under some trees. He would walk to one tree with his head toward the ground, then turn and walk back to the other tree. He continued to do this over and over. I noticed he was wearing a jacket that looked familiar to me. I knew that Paul had a jacket like that. I thought: *Surely, that kid can't be Paul?* I was so intrigued by what I saw until I pulled over to the curb, stopped my car, and watched. He continued to walk from one tree then back to another tree. I got out of my car and walked out on the schoolyard. The walk from my car to where he was took about two minutes. It was Paul, and he was so engrossed in what he was doing that he did not see me as I approached him. I walked within just a few feet from him, when suddenly he saw me, he was shocked. I asked him, "What are you doing?"

He said, "I'm just out here praying."

I said, "Do you come out here often?"

"Yes, I come out here every day," he replied.

Then looking at the other kids playing ball I said, "Why don't you play ball with the others?"

He looked at me apologetically and said, "They don't want me to play with them, I'm not a good ball player and nobody wants me on their team." Then he added, "So, I just come out here by myself and pray every day." I was stunned.

I left him there under the trees and continued my trip downtown. I could not get this incident off my mind. When I got home, I told his mother what I had witnessed, and of course it upset her also. That event bothered me so much that I made an appointment with the principal. I shared my experience and told the principal: "You have a great school, and you pride yourself in it. However, there is an area of your program that has holes in it." He was shocked that I would say such a thing. I let him know that I did not think too much of a school that would allow a student, any student, to feel completely rejected by his peers simply because he was from Mississippi. This is a devastating experience for any child and they should not have to go through it. He listened to me with real concern.

The principal really wanted to help. He offered some quick thoughts and some possible solutions. He said he would continue to give his full attention to the matter and do all that he could to find something that was workable. He assured me that the problem would be thoroughly addressed.

In the meantime, I continued to be burdened about it. In a Sunday evening service, I asked our church to help us pray about it. I shared only a small bit of information with them, because I wanted them to know only enough to help us pray. Paul was embarrassed for the church to know anything at all about it. I did not want to embarrass him, but we needed help, and we needed it fast.

After the church prayed with us over the matter, the very next week, an exchange student from Mexico, enrolled in the school. He was a jolly, cute little boy with a glowing personality. All the students thought he was special, and they all wanted to be his friend. He lived with a very influential family in Webster Groves. He could have chosen any student in the school as his best friend, but of all the students in the school, he chose Paul to be his best friend.

One night as we returned home from an engagement, my car lights shined on a young boy sitting on a tree stump in the churchyard. I asked, "Who in the world is that?" Paul spoke up and said, "That's Wilfredo Vargas from Mexico."

He had been sitting there waiting for Paul to return home. He came inside our house for all of us to meet him. From that night on, he was at our house constantly. Wilfredo called Paul several times each day. When he called, he would say, "Is Paul?" The other kids invited Wilfredo to their parties and social events, but he would not go without Paul. So, they had to invite Paul if they wanted Wilfredo. Paul's social life picked up dramatically after Wilfredo arrived. I really do believe prayer had a lot to do with it.

At the close of Paul's eighth grade year, I came home from the office very late one night, and as I got into bed I saw a letter on the nightstand. It was addressed simply, "Daddy." I picked it up and saw that it contained several pages. I thought, *I'm so tired tonight, I'll read this in the morning*. I laid it back down and started to turn off the light when suddenly I felt I needed to read it right then!

As I began to read the letter, I was moved to tears. It was one of the most heart-wrenching letters I had ever read. Paul was pleading with me to allow him to go back to Mississippi and live with my sister Dianne. He told me how much he loved his mother and me; how much he loved his brothers and sister, but he hated his school, and he did not want to go to Webster Groves High School the following year. He so feared the taunts and ugly remarks from other students that he could hardly stand it. He told me how he had hated every day of school at Clark and Hixon. He said, "I was little, and I had to go." He told me I could whip him or do anything I wanted to, but he was not going to go to Webster Groves High. "I will run away from home if you try to make me go to that high school," he continued.

I knew that he was very serious about what he said. It was not like Paul to say these kinds of things. I realized that the problem I thought was better was not much better after all. It only appeared to be improved. He had kept it to himself and had not told us what he was going through. The ridicule about his Southern roots, the way he talked, and even about his church was more than he could tolerate. He had had enough, and he just wanted out of it!

I did not want Paul to leave us and move back to Mississippi. I could not stand for him to do that. I know that my sister would have welcomed him and would have treated him as her own child, but he was my son. I loved him, and I did not want him to be away from us. The rest of the family felt the same way. No one in the family had knowledge of what he was going through. It was bad, really bad, and something would have to be done about it one way or another. I made up my mind that night that unless there was a change in Paul's school situation I would have to resign the church and move, and I really did not want to do that either. It does not matter how well you are succeeding in your life, if your child is that unhappy, you have to do something about it.

I was deeply troubled, and I did not know what to do. This was a very big problem for us, and we needed help. This time I would not tell the church. This time we would do the praying ourselves. I did not know anyone to go to for help. I did not know anyone in the high school administration. There was no one for us to turn to except the Lord. We did not know how it would work out, but we prayed. During the summer there came a change in Paul's attitude toward the high school. When the time came, he enrolled without a problem and began the year as if there was no concern at all. To our delight, we soon discovered that the high school students were more mature and they did not resort to the childish slurs and barbs as the lower classes did. Also Paul was now more mature himself, and he could handle those things much better than before.

Paul's high school years actually became his best years in the Webster Groves school system. Perhaps the class structure, new facility, and new faculty may have all contributed. It appeared that he was able to finish his high school years with much less stress and difficulty than he had experienced before.

In his junior year, he made the decision to play football. He always wanted to be involved in sports but never had the right opportunity. With his school years coming to an end soon, he made the decision to try out for the team. He did this with full knowledge that it would be very difficult for him to make the team. He had never played football and most everyone on the team had played since elementary school. St. Louis County has a great program for developing football players called the Junior Football League, or JFL. Paul had never been involved in the JFL program or anything else, so he had to start from scratch. However, he had the desire and he was determined to go out for the team, regardless of the odds against him. I guess he figured that all his life he had had to overcome odds, this would be no different.

He gave it his best effort and stayed with it, even though he saw very little playing time. His senior year gave him opportunity for more playing time, and he was thrilled and excited each time he got in a game. He enjoyed the game, and enjoyed being a member of his high school team. Webster Groves had a great football team in 1984 and 1985. A highlight for Paul as a senior was when Webster Groves and Kirkwood played each other in Bush Stadium. He enjoyed most of his senior year more than any other year in school.

In his junior and senior years, many of his classmates began to discover that Paul had tremendous musical ability, and their attitude toward him changed. He began to feel accepted, and that helped him overcome some of the hurts and disappointments he had endured over the past years. He began to play music with a group from his school. They actually became fairly good together and were featured in several appearances; which he called "gigs."

At the same time, he continued to make a significant contribution to our church music program. In addition to his ability to play six musical instruments, he began to take solo vocal parts in cantatas and special singing programs. God really patted him on the back and blessed him with great musical talent; talent which he unselfishly used and dedicated to the Lord.

But even in the church there was resentment by some who felt he was too young to be given choice parts.

After struggling to find acceptance by his peers in school, Paul graduated from Webster Groves High School on June 6, 1985. Just like other things that had happened to him through most of his life, it rained on his graduation day, and the activities had to be moved from the football field into a crowded gymnasium. As a result, seating was limited to the immediate family members only. Some of our family from Mississippi were unable to see him graduate, which disappointed him greatly. It is truly sad that a person with his abilities, talent, and character missed out on so much of what life could have afforded him.

After graduation, Paul decided that he wanted to attend a junior college in Mississippi. I was opposed to the idea until he told me it was because he had never been able to attend any school that I attended. He wanted to attend Pearl River Junior College in Poplarville, Mississippi, because I had graduated from there in 1959. How could I refuse him after that?

The time came for him to enroll, and the entire family traveled to Mississippi with him as he prepared for college. I accompanied him for his registration. While on campus we met some of my schoolmates who offered to help Paul any way they could. President Marvin White personally welcomed Paul to Pearl River, which made him feel really good.

The following day we left him at my sister's home and made our way back for Sunday duties at the church. I shall never forget how Paul stood outside and watched us drive away. He continued to watch until we were completely out of sight.

Returning home without him was a strange and difficult experience. I experienced such loneliness that I could hardly stand it, often breaking out in tears. My wife became very concerned for me and could not understand what was going on. I look back and wonder if perhaps that was a foreshadow of things to come. It took me some time to adjust to his being away from us.

He enrolled and completed his freshman year. During that year, he spent much of his time at our homeplace located in the country just a few miles from the college. He loved the outdoors, hunting and fishing. He spent as much of his time enjoying that as he could. He killed his first deer, and happily brought some of the venison home to St. Louis. He had a passion for flying, and he would fly home on Southwest or Ozark Airlines every opportunity he could find. Of course, we were always happy when he came home.

Because he knew how much I wanted him to stay at home, he enrolled at Meramic Community College in St. Louis the following year. Again, I was with him for his interview with the director of the Music Department. He was asked to play the piano for the professor. He had not brought any music with him, so Paul just sat down at the piano and began playing without music. He played for quite some time before the professor stopped him. He had allowed Paul to play longer than usual because he enjoyed his style of playing. The professor made several positive comments concerning Paul's ability and welcomed him into the school. Paul took several music classes and sang in the college choir while at Meramic.

Even though he did well at Meramic, he was restless. He was an unfulfilled young man. His dream was to become a firefighter. A dream that only he really knew and understood. But a dream that continually drove him and motivated him. A dream that would come true for him one day, but a dream that carried grave consequences.

Chapter 5

The End of a Dream

What makes a person choose to become a firefighter? Is it the glamour? Is it the challenge? Is it the excitement and flow of adrenaline? Is it the pay? I am not sure about the first three, but I feel comfortable in saying it is definitely not the latter. In my opinion, firefighters are not paid anywhere close to what they deserve for the service they perform and the ever-present danger they face.

Firefighters are people; they are real flesh and blood. They are sons and daughters, husbands and wives. They are brothers and sisters, fathers and mothers. They have real emotions; they laugh; they cry; they care very deeply for others. They share a special bond with fellow firefighters. When an alarm comes in, they are instantly transformed into fearless "Angels of Mercy" who willingly place themselves on the front lines of danger. Yet they seek no glory and do not consider themselves heroes.

I believe that people are born with certain characteristics that greatly influence their lives in later years. A true firefighter is born with a servant's spirit. Their greatest fulfillment comes by serving others. It is almost like a calling on their lives, and they can do nothing else. They are unselfish, brave, and dedicated. The general public has little knowledge of the sacrifice firefighters make, their level of dedication, and the training they go through to become firefighters. Serving others can be the only reason that every day on their jobs they willingly place their lives on the line. I have found this to be true regardless if they are structural or wildlands firefighters. I deeply regret I did not understand this until after Paul's death.

Why did Paul dream of becoming a firefighter from an early age? I am not sure that I can give an answer. There was something within him that motivated him and gave him the desire to become a firefighter. Even as a child he had an interest in firefighting. He loved little fire trucks and enjoyed playing fireman. When he was a kid, his favorite television program was "Emergency." He never missed an episode. After each program, he wanted to act out the story with his younger sister and brother.

While serving as pastor of a church in Jackson, Mississippi, two members of our church —Billy Bush and Curtis Clark—were captains in the Jackson Fire Department. Paul almost idolized them. He picked their brains about firefighting, and he even tried to imitate them. On a visit to a fire station, Captain Billy Bush took Paul and me up in the snorkel for an aboveground view. The experience made me very nervous, but I think it only added to Paul's already strong interest in becoming a firefighter.

When Paul was a senior in high school, he informed me that Chief Entrekin of the Webster Groves, Missouri, Fire Department promised him a job when he graduated. He was thrilled and excited; but I am sorry that I did not share his enthusiasm at that time. I just did not understand how important it was to him.

My family made a move to Greenville, Mississippi, in March 1987. At the time of our move, Paul made the decision to remain in St. Louis. I did not really want him to stay behind, and I did not understand why he wanted to stay, but I accepted it—

if that was what he wanted. Our family has always been close, and I questioned why he did not want to move with us to Mississippi. I now know the real reason he wanted to stay behind. He still had high hopes for a position with the Webster Groves Fire Department. As much as he would miss his family, his desire to become a firefighter was so great that he was willing to face the loneliness and inconvenience of being away from his family.

Paul helped us make the move to Greenville but returned to St. Louis within a few days. We were busy getting settled into the new church, which occupied much of our time and attention. Yet we missed Paul; it was just not the same for us with him away. His sister Dawn was away at school in Tennessee, and our nest was becoming empty.

A few months passed when our phone rang around two o'clock in the morning. For a pastor, that is always a troubling experience. It usually means that somebody is in trouble and they are in need of the pastor. We did not have a caller ID at the time; in fact, I am not sure they even existed then. I had no idea who was calling, but I felt sure it was someone with some bad news. I slowly picked up the receiver and said, "Hello." It was Paul on the other end of the line who blurted out, "Daddy, what are you doing?"

I answered, "I was sleeping until the phone woke me. What are you doing this time of the morning?"

"Nothing much," was his reply. Then he asked, "Daddy, would it be all right if I moved back to Mississippi with you?"

I said, "Of course it would Paul, we would be happy."

Then he said, "I've been thinking about it, and I think that I will."

I asked, "When do you plan to move?"

He answered, "Now."

Puzzled, I asked, "Where are you?"

He answered, "I'm in Clarksdale." Clarksdale is in the Mississippi Delta, just over an hour's drive from Greenville.

I said, "All right Paul, come on home. We will be waiting for you." He arrived just about daybreak, and I could tell he was happy to be back with us. I surely was happy to have him back home. He continued to live with us and brought us much happiness.

After moving back to Mississippi, he proudly announced one day that the chief of the Greenville Fire Department had offered him a job. Again, his enthusiasm was overflowing; he was thrilled beyond words. I congratulated him, but I must admit I did not feel the excitement that he felt. To him it was a dream come true; something he had waited for all his life.

He literally threw himself into becoming the best firefighter that he was capable of becoming. He studied, did his physical exercises, and trained hard. He took advantage of every opportunity for training that was available. Training Officer Eugene Doss stated, "Paul was just starving to death for training, you know, 'show me something, show me something.'"

Training Officer Lieutenant Felix Zanders directed Paul's immediate basic training with the local department. He attended the Mississippi State Fire Academy in Jackson and completed the Firefighters 1001 course. He completed the Firefighters 1002 course soon afterwards. He later enrolled in EMT training offered by Mississippi Delta Community College. He completed that course on Thursday prior to his accident on Sunday morning.

I believe Paul felt a degree of satisfaction upon the completion of each training course. However, he never made a big deal of it to us. I never thought too much about it until I was invited to speak at the Metro Fire Chiefs Convention in April 2000. I boarded my flight in Atlanta on my way to Miami. I had a window seat on the Boeing 767; the adjacent aisle seat was unoccupied. Soon a handsome young man sat down beside me. He was talkative and immediately engaged me in conversation. "Do you live in Miami?" he asked.

I replied, "No, I am going there to speak to a convention of fire chiefs."

To which he responded, "Oh, you're a fire chief."

"No, I am not," I said.

"Are you a firefighter," he asked? Being a minister I wanted to answer "Yes, I do fight fire," but I said, "No."

With a puzzled expression, he asked, "Then why are you going to speak to fire chiefs?"

I told him that my son was a firefighter and was killed in the line of duty. I had been invited to share his story at the convention. With that he proceeded to tell me of his brother-in-law's graduation from the Dade County, Florida, Fire Academy the week before. He was very excited about his brother-in-law becoming a firefighter. He told me about how the entire family gathered together and celebrated the graduation and what a big event it was for them.

I sat in stunned silence thinking that we never celebrated any of Paul's graduations or accomplishments with the fire department. They just happened and nothing much was even said about it. It wasn't because we were not proud of him and happy for him, because we were. It was simply because we did not understand the fire service and how important these things were to him. How I wish we had celebrated with him, especially his graduating EMT school, but we did not. I live with that regret continually.

Paul enjoyed being a member of the crew of Captain Ronnie Criswell, Engineer Kenny Cole, and himself. He believed in his crew and in the leadership of Captain Criswell, and Paul treasured their time in service. The crew was dismantled when Captain Criswell retired from the department and Kenny Cole was promoted to Lieutenant. Paul was assigned to a new crew and worked in various stations in the city over the next few months. His last assignment was with Lieutenant Melvin Jackson and Engineer Jerry Jordan at Station Two.

Some of my cherished memories are his calling home and asking what we were having for dinner. He loved his mother's cooking and wanted someone to bring him a plate of whatever we were having. Of course we did each time he called. I visited almost every firehouse in the city with his dinner until they thought we were his private caterers. I do not regret one time having done that for him.

Thanksgiving

In 1989, our family made plans to spend Thanksgiving at our farm in South Mississippi. Paul was required to work with his shift beginning Thanksgiving evening; therefore, he would not be able to make the trip with us. We could have stayed in Greenville, which would have allowed him to have dinner with the family. If I had even dreamed what was about to happen, we certainly would have stayed.

We planned for a week of hunting—just the two of us—following Thanksgiving. He made arrangements with his superiors for a few days off, and he and I would spend that time together hunting at our farm. As our family drove to Poplarville, Paul followed behind us in his car. We did some Christmas shopping in Jackson, and he spent some time shopping with us. After shopping, we ate at a fast-food restaurant and left. I recall how he looked at us with such a mournful expression as we drove away, leaving him behind in Jackson.

The family spent Thanksgiving without him that year; it was the first time we had ever done that. I really did not enjoy that day very much, it was not the same without Paul with us. That was the first time, and now we spend each Thanksgiving without him. It makes for a very lonely time.

My wife and the children returned to Greenville after Thanksgiving, and Paul was to join me at the farm after he completed his duty shift. I was looking forward to the time he and I would spend together, as well as getting in some good hunting. I was so excited that I could hardly wait for him to join me. It would have been a rare treat for us both, but it was never to be.

I spent the night alone and went into the woods very early the next morning. When I returned to the house a few hours later, I found notes posted all over my door. I was informed that I needed to call the church immediately. I made the call and was told that a member of the church had been hospitalized. I changed my plans at once and left for Greenville. Of course, Paul would not leave Greenville due to the circumstances.

When I walked into the hospital room, the church member was making an amazing recovery. The local hospital did some further tests, then transferred him to a Jackson hospital. He underwent additional tests in Jackson and was released from the hospital.

Because our plans were interrupted, Paul continued to work and did not take the time off as planned. As a result, he was in rotation to work the shift beginning at 5:00 p.m. on December 2 and ending at 5:00 p.m. on December 3. This placed him on duty on that fateful Sunday morning of December 3, 1989. Had he joined me in Poplarville as planned, we would have enjoyed the time together. He would not have been working on the day of that fire, and perhaps things would have turned out differently.

December 2, 1989

Paul worked at almost every station in the city, but he enjoyed working at Number Two Station best because it was the one that saw the most action. He liked what he did and wanted to be where the action was. He was working at that station on December 2, 1989, when his shift commander, Lieutenant Jackson called in sick.

Assistant chief, Major Billy Thomas, made the decision to close Station Number Two and move Paul and Jerry Jordan to Central Station. This was the beginning of a series of blunders and bad decisions that I believe resulted in Paul's death. Apparently that move was made to avoid bringing in another officer for Station Two and paying overtime. Whatever the reason, it was a move that sealed Paul's fate.

After moving the two firefighters from Station Two to Central Station, they were assigned new duties. Paul was assigned to the rescue squad, commanded by Captain Bob Moore. He took his assignment on the rescue squad very seriously. He immediately began to perform his duties with true professionalism.

Paul was one of the most compassionate people that I have ever known. He was always pulling for the underdog, the less fortunate in life. His heart went out to anyone in need. Maybe it was because of things he encountered in his own life that made him want to reach out to those who were hurting. His former training officer, Lieutenant Zanders, said: "Paul was one of the best people anyone would ever want to meet. Everybody liked Paul. He would do anything he could for anybody!"

According to the testimony of his fellow workers who were on the scene, a call came in at approximately 10:10 p.m. on December 2. Station Five responded to the Saturday night house fire at 1920 Michigan Street. Rescue Nine was also dispatched to the same fire along with Engine Number Seven.

The arriving crews quickly attacked the fire, and it was soon extinguished. There was a little dog in the house that was overcome by smoke and was in a dying condition. After the fire was brought under control, Paul took the dog aside and worked to revive it. As the firefighters left the scene, the dog was on his feet and in good shape. Ironically, only a few hours later, Paul would be the one needing resuscitation.

December 3, 1989

At approximately 8:58 on Sunday morning, December 3, 1989, a call came into dispatch that a dumpster was burning at 516 Walker Street. Engine Number Three, commanded by Lieutenant Willie Wallace with Engineer Sonny Lee and Firefighter Larry Newton, was dispatched to the scene. Immediately, Rescue Nine commanded by Captain Bob Moore with Engineer Jerry Jordan and Firefighter Paul Smith was dispatched from Central Station as backup.

Engine Number Three arrived on the scene first. Upon arriving, they discovered that it was not a dumpster on fire; rather it was a two-story apartment building. Lieutenant Wallace assessed the fire and made a determination that it was just "light moderate smoke or light moderate flames inside the building." The main source of the fire was actually at the rear of the building, something he failed to determine.

His plan of attack was to lay a 125-psi line into the building to extinguish the fire. Firefighter Newton began removing the line, and Lieutenant Wallace took the nozzle and moved toward the entrance of the building. At the entrance of the building, Firefighter Paul Smith, who had arrived on Rescue Nine, joined him. Wallace led Smith into the building and up the stairs. Later Newton followed the line and joined them on the second floor.

Newton stated that when he arrived on the second floor, Lieutenant Wallace and another firefighter, whom he did not recognize at the time, were searching for the location of the fire. Within a short time, smoke and heat filled the area until it became very difficult to see. As the heat and smoke became more intense, Lieutenant Wallace said something was wrong with his air pack and he was going down. He left the two young firefighters alone, unsupervised, in a very volatile situation. I am told that a cardinal rule for fire officers is that they never leave their men alone in a fire. They make sure each firefighter is accounted for before they exit themselves. Paul had less than two years service with the department and Newton had only five months. According to Newton, it started getting very hot and he said to Paul, "Let's get out of here."

Paul responded, "I can't find the fire. Where is the fire?"

Newton said, "It kept getting hotter and hotter, and I said, 'Let's get out of here." Newton then turned and began exiting the building, thinking that Paul was behind him. As he moved down the first flight of stairs, he was met with a strong blast of flames and extreme heat that had broken through a hole in the wall. Thinking, *I'll never get pass that,* he turned around and started back up the stairs. The heat at the top of the stairs was so intense that he decided to turn around and attempt to rush past the blasting flames. Somehow he made it outside where he saw Lieutenant Wallace standing on the grounds.

Wallace asked, "Where is Paul?"

Looking behind him, Newton realized that Paul did not follow him down the stairs. Newton responded, "He's still up there. We've got to get a ladder or something and get him out." Wallace just stood there and did nothing. Newton said, "Man, we need to do something." Newton then went out to the truck and told Engineer Lee, "Paul didn't come down and is still in the building."

Lee then yelled to Captain Bo Gentry, who was walking across the lawn, "Paul is still in the building." *

According to interviews with a number of firefighters, once outside the building, Lieutenant Wallace did nothing himself. One captain said, "Wallace fiddled with the air packs, then went to the truck and messed with a ladder, just killing time." At some point, Wallace did make a call on his radio of a "possible victim down." The officers in the department said they never related that call as a "firefighter down" call.

Captain Gentry was working the fire at the rear of the building with his crew from Station One. Moving to the front of the building, he saw an inch and three-quarter line going up the stairs in the front of the building. He knew the fire was in the back of the building, but realizing if the line went up the stairs, that was where the men would be. So, he and rookie firefighter, Tim Dodson, put on their air packs and started to go up the stairs. They went up the first flight of stairs to the landing where the blast had broken through the wall. When they approached that area, they too were hit by the strong blast of heat and smoke. They had no visibility at all, Dodson said, "It was getting too hot for me, and I wanted to get out."

Captain Gentry saw the line going upstairs and thought, "I need to put a little water on this fire." He gave the line a yank; there was no resistance. It was the line Paul was holding when Newton last saw him. Gentry knew that no one was holding the line, so he pulled it down to himself and began to hit the fire with water. He soon realized it was not a small fire, but a much bigger fire than he first thought. After putting a sufficient amount of water on the fire, he dropped the line and turned and went outside the building.

When he got outside the building, Lieutenant Wallace told him that Paul was still inside. Gentry replied, "Still in the building?"

"Yes," said Wallace. "I think we can get him with a ladder from the second story window."

There was plywood over the second story windows and Gentry thought, *We don't have time to get a ladder, pry plywood from the windows, and attempt a rescue. It has to be done now.* He reasoned to himself, *Paul is probably up there, stumbling around, trying to find a window to get out.*

Captain Gentry told Wallace, "We're wasting time here. I'm going in to get him. I'm going to see if I can find him and get him out of there."

Determined to do what he could to reach his fellow comrade, Bo Gentry reentered the building. He reached the stairs and began to climb. As he climbed toward the top, he knew, by the amount of heat he was feeling, that it was not going to be good when he found Paul. More concerned for Paul that he was his own safety, Captain Gentry pushed himself onward. As he moved to the top of the stairs, he thought, *I've got to get in there and find him because I can't stand much of this myself.* Gentry estimated the heat to be at least a thousand degrees.

The fire was fully involved when Gentry reached the top floor. A standard search procedure for firefighters is to perform a right-hand search pattern. They get in a crawl position and move in a circle to their right side. On his knees, crawling in total darkness, Gentry turned to his left rather than to his right. Wallace had said Paul was up there, and could be reached from the windows. So, Gentry moved in the direction of the windows. Feeling his way along, he bumped into Paul's feet. He couldn't see him, but he reached down and felt his fireman's boots and knew that it was Paul. Paul was not moving!

He grabbed him under his arms, but Paul's air pack, still on his back, made the effort very difficult. Gentry pulled him through the door and down the stairs backwards. He did not have time to pick and choose which kind of drag or carry was best to use. He was burning himself, and he knew Paul had to be removed from the building at once. Grabbing him under his arms and pulling him backwards, he brought him down both flights of stairs. At that point, Gentry was completely exhausted. He just could not carry him anymore. But, he had reached the door before he stopped.

Captain Bob Moore saw Gentry with Paul and ran to them. He assisted in getting Paul clear of the building and on the ground. Paul was not breathing. Gentry told Bingham to get the oxygen off the rescue truck. They removed Paul's helmet. As he looked at Paul, his face and his jet black hair, Gentry thought, *If his hair is not burned, maybe his lungs are not burned too badly.*

Once his helmet was removed, they attempted to revive Paul. One firefighter gave him a few breaths. Larry Grayson gave him a couple of chest compressions, after which Paul took one great big breath. Captain Gentry called on his walkie-talkie, "Fireman down! We need an ambulance."

The dispatcher, having heard the radio chatter, had concluded that the person down was Paul Smith and had already called for an ambulance. The ambulance arrived within seconds of Paul's first breath. Paramedic Lamar Gardner, took over the patient at that time.

Paul was placed in the ambulance and transported to the Delta Medical Center Emergency Unit. As fate would have it, Captain Gentry was also a part-time ambulance driver. He volunteered to drive the ambulance to the hospital to allow the paramedic to be with Paul. Upon arrival at the hospital, Paul was placed in the cardiac room, and Gentry helped get him undressed for the examination. At that time, the pressure of it all hit him really hard, and he had to get out of the trauma unit as quickly as he could. He returned to the fire scene and continued his duties there.

Dr. Robert Argo treated Paul in the Emergency Room. He was intubated and initially diagnosed with third-degree burns on his face and second-degree burns on both hands. After two IVs were started and the routine lab work was completed, he was admitted to the Burn Unit under the care of Dr. Robert Bowman, who had visited him in the Emergency Room.

* *Author's note:* It seems that what happened to Paul was a "flashover" or a "rollover." Experts who have studied reports and documentation of the fire believe Paul was caught in a rollover and immediately knocked unconscious. A *rollover* is "the fire coming up over the top and the super-heated gases mixed with oxygen ignite, producing a violent combustion." They are convinced the combustion produced such velocity and force that Paul took a couple of deep hits of smoke and gas and that was it—he was down for the count. Paul was still alive but unconscious and unable to escape the intense heat about him. He could have been rescued had he not been left alone, or if an immediate rescue effort had been initiated.

Chapter 6

The Day of The Tragedy

It was Sunday morning, December 3, 1989. The weather was colder than usual for the Mississippi Delta. As was my custom, I would be in my office no later than eight o'clock each Sunday morning to prepare for the worship service. That Sunday would be no different. I arrived at the church around eight o'clock, checked the heat throughout the building, then went into my office to review notes, check last minute details, and to meditate. It was during that time I heard the sound of sirens breaking the silence of the cold morning. A number of emergency vehicles moved rapidly across the little delta city of Greenville. I didn't think too much of it at first, but as I noticed more and more sirens filling the air with their mournful, wailing sounds, I wondered what this could be? I thought, *This must be something really big*. I had no way of knowing just how big it would be for us on that fateful morning.

I heard some people enter the church and gather in the foyer. I was not disturbed, so I continued my activity until I heard an unfamiliar voice asking if the pastor was in. He was directed to my office. As I opened the door, standing before me was the local fire chief. His uniform was wet and soiled, his hair was out of place, and he looked at me with a frightened look on his face. "We had a fire this morning, and Paul's been hurt," he said. "Will you please come go with me?" I told the people who had already arrived for church that I was going with the chief, but I would be back shortly.

We got into the chief's red car. He turned on the red lights and the siren, and we went speeding down the streets. We wove in and out of traffic, around other automobiles, through red lights and stop signs, and traveled at a rather fast speed toward the hospital. The chief looked straight ahead as he drove and never said anything to me. I asked, "Is Paul hurt very badly?" He replied, "I'm afraid it's pretty bad," and continued to drive, looking straight ahead. We soon came to the hospital, and he drove to the emergency area. Getting out of his car and walking into the emergency room was a chore itself. Inside the emergency waiting area were a number of stabbing and cutting victims from the Saturday night before. A couple of women were about to give birth, and more than a few others with various medical problems were all lined up to see a doctor. I tried to negotiate my way through the crowd to a line formed in front of a desk where a receptionist was seated. From her appearance, her Saturday night must have been wild also. I stood in the line for a moment before I decided to move up and asked about Paul. Identifying myself, I told the receptionist that the injured firefighter brought in earlier was my son and I would like to see him. She told me to go back to the end of the line and wait my turn. I must tell you that I was most surprised by what she said, but I did return to the end of the line of about ten people to wait.

At this time, I did not know where the fire chief was. He left me alone at the hospital. In retrospect, I believe he was in a state of shock himself and was unable to stay with me. Perhaps he was needed at the fire scene, I really don't know. But oh, how much I needed someone from the Fire Department with me during that time. If the chief was not able to stay with me himself, it would have been helpful to me if he had assigned someone else. Somehow, I just cannot believe I would have gone though the terrible ordeal that I went through if a member of the Fire Department had been present. But I was alone, so I had to make the best of it.

I waited in the line about two or three minutes, and it never moved at all. By that time, I was getting impatient and very concerned about what was going on with Paul. I moved back to the receptionist and said: "I really need to know what is going on with my son. Is there anyone who can talk with me?" It was pretty obvious by this time that she was more than a little annoyed with me. She raised her voice and scolded me before everyone in the waiting area. She told me that I was no better than anyone else in there. She said that some of those people had been waiting for a long time and I could not jump ahead of them. "Go back to the end of the line and wait like I told you," she yelled. I felt that every eye in that huge room was looking right at me. I was so embarrassed and humiliated, I wanted to run and hide. I was the pastor of a rather large church in the city; some of these people knew me. I did not want to create a scene, so I went back to the end of the line. But as I stood there waiting, I became upset. I thought, *Why did the chief drive so fast through red lights and stop signs to get me here if all I can do is wait?* I went back to the desk and spoke in a tone of voice that got her attention. "Listen, young lady," I said, "I came here to see about my son, the firefighter, and I want somebody to tell me something, or I am going back there myself, right now!" This time her reply was softer, and she told me to go through a door into the hallway. Walk so far, make a turn and I would see a little room. I should wait in that room until someone came to speak with me.

I made my way as she instructed and walked to the little room. Above the door was the word "Chapel." Having been in the ministry, visiting hospitals with families through the years, taught me what that meant. Now I really became concerned. I was there alone, and no one came to talk with me. I tried to sit, but I could not remain seated. All I could do was walk around and around in the little chapel and wait. So I waited, and I waited, and no one came to tell me anything. I noticed a telephone there, so I thought I needed to call my family. They did not know what was going on. Our son, Joey, answered the phone. I told him where I was, that his brother had been hurt, and to get his mother and little brother and come to the hospital. I told him that I did not think Paul's injuries were serious, but for them come to the hospital as soon as they could. "Be sure you do not upset your mother," I said. They came to the hospital as fast as they could and wanted to know how Paul was, but I did not know anything to tell them. Finally, a nurse came into the chapel and talked with us very briefly. She spoke in very general terms, nothing specific. Her message was mostly that the doctor was almost finished in the ER and that he would be in to talk with us as soon as he could. She then left us, and we continued to wait alone.

The doctor finally came in to talk with us. The expression on his face told me he would rather be doing almost anything rather than talking to us about our son. He lived in our neighborhood, and no doubt had seen

Paul running past his house during his physical fitness exercises. He talked to us in medical terms that we really did not understand. "We've finished in the ER, and I am going to admit him to the burn unit," he said. The Mississippi Firefighters Memorial Burn Unit was connected with this particular hospital in Greenville. When he said that they were going to admit him to the burn unit, that was the first clue I had that Paul had been burned. The chief said he had been hurt, but I did not equate being hurt with being burned. Maybe he fell from a ladder, maybe something fell on him, or maybe a vehicle hit him, I thought. But I never thought that he had been burned. I do not know why, but it just never crossed my mind that he had been burned.

I asked if we could see him, but the doctor said that we really could not at that time. The doctor explained that it would take some time for the burn unit to do all the things necessary for Paul when he was first admitted. After all those things were completed, we would be allowed to see him. Again we did not know how severe his burns were, we only knew he was burned. He then told us that the burn unit had a waiting room on the other side of the hospital, it was a considerable distance from the ER. He told us to follow a nurse who would lead us to the area where we could wait until they called us to see him. He told us that all the family, the four of us, would be permitted to go in together for the first visit. Following our initial visit, the hospital would allow only two visitors at a time during regular visiting hours. My wife and I with our two sons Joey, age 18, and Stevie, age 11, would be the first visitors. Our daughter, Dawn, was in her senior year at Lee College, located in Cleveland, Tennessee. At that time, she did not know anything about her brother's injury.

We followed the nurse who led us through the emergency area, and as we passed the trauma rooms, we noticed a flurry of activity with several nurses quickly positioning themselves before a large glass-enclosed room to shield us from seeing the patient inside. I later learned the patient was our son. We passed through the trauma area and reached a long hallway, then we turned right. Making the long walk to the end of the hallway, we came to one door that opened straight ahead into the burn unit and another door on the left side which opened into the waiting area.

As we entered a rather large waiting area, we were chilled by the temperature of the room. There was no one else in there at the time. I later learned the families of other patients in the burn center did not wait in the waiting room. They knew the visiting hours, and rather than sit around in that room, they would leave and go other places, returning at the next visiting time. The nurse left us in the waiting room and returned to the ER, and once again we were alone. We tried to comfort each other, but we did not know how. We did not know what to say to each other. We did not even know what was wrong with Paul, so how could we console each other? We just waited and wondered and prayed.

Then I remembered that my church did not know where I was or what was going on. It was now past time to begin church services, and no doubt they were wondering why I was not there. I needed to call them, but there was no telephone in that area. There was a receptionist's desk, but there was no receptionist or telephone. I knew where one was—in the little room where we had been waiting. I decided to go to back to the chapel and call the church from there. I made my way into the long corridor to go back through the hospital emergency area to the telephone in the chapel. I turned right and walked almost half the length of the corridor when a group of nurses came out of the trauma area with a patient on a gurney. They turned toward me, so I moved to one side of the corridor to give them room to pass. I cannot explain what happened next or why. Just as they got even with me, the patient on the gurney suddenly sat up. The nurses stopped pushing the gurney and stood still. When the patient sat up, I was shocked at the sight before me; I could not believe my eyes. I could hardly recognize this was a human being he looked so terrible. I thought, *Whoever this poor person is he is in real trouble.* Then a nurse spoke words that sent chills down my spine and caused my heart to jump into my throat. She said, "Lay back down, Paul." I stood there stunned! I could not move. I did not even recognize my own son. It was a horrible experience—one that still gives me nightmares, even to this day.

Paul did not respond to their command to lie down, rather, he continued to sit upright on the gurney looking straight ahead, making no other movement. It was as if he knew I was there close by and was waiting for me to step over to the gurney and somehow make everything all right again. All his life Paul seemed to believe that his daddy could do what no one else could do. He thought I could fix anything and do anything. He held me in higher esteem than I ever deserved. During his lifetime, I had cleaned his cuts and scratches, rubbed his bruises, and kissed his wounds. I had stayed at his bed in hospitals, and I had listened to his problems. I always did everything I could to comfort him and ease his pain. But this time I could not do anything for him; I was helpless. I wish so much that I had at least gone over to him and put my hand on his arm. I wish I had said something to him, just anything. But I did not; I just froze there in absolute horror. This has haunted me through the years, and I have had to deal with it the best that I can. Once again the nurse said, "Lay down, Paul." This time he did. Slowly and silently, he lay back down on the gurney, and they continued to roll him toward the burn unit. I just stood speechless and watched them as they rolled him through the doors, which slowly closed behind him. I did not know that this would be the last time I would ever see my son move.

I cannot explain the feeling that came over me at that time. I do not know if I went into shock, panic, or just what happened to me, but I could not continue to go make the phone call. I had to get back to my family. I needed them now as I had never needed them before. So I turned and walked back to the waiting area. I paused at the doorway and talked to myself. I could not go in and let them see me cry or appear upset. *I've got to be strong for their sake,* I thought, *I can't let them know how badly Paul is burned.* So I took a couple of deep breaths; I counted to ten; I regained my composure, or so I thought; and I went back into the waiting room. When my family saw me, they immediately knew something terrible was wrong. I had not spoken a word. Maybe it was my expression or the color of my face or something, but they knew. I could not deceive them; I had to tell them that he was hurt very, very badly, and we must pray hard for him. So we huddled together there in the cold waiting room of the burn center. There was no one with us from the Fire Department, no one from the hospital, and no one from our church because they did not know about it yet. It was just the four of us—my wife, Joey, Stevie, and me—and no more. We were alone. I will never forget how alone I felt at that time. I will never forget how hopeless I felt. It was a terrible nightmare!

Some time passed before some of the members of our church figured out that something must be wrong, and a few of the men came looking for us. Norman Barrentine and Tony Johnson came in and stayed with us most of the day. As I recall, Norman remained close at my side eager to do anything he could for us. I was numb from shock at the time, but some things are etched forever in my mind.

Greenville is a river town where gossip flows faster than the mighty Mississippi River, which flows past her shores. The news spread over the town, and soon the waiting area was filled with people—church members, members of the Fire Department, city officials, and a number of people who were just curious. The hospital brought a telephone into the waiting area and connected it. Immediately, it began ringing, and it rang continually. The news spread quickly across the state and many friends, fellow pastors, and family members soon began to call. I would hang up the phone from one conversation, and right away it would ring again.

About two hours passed before they allowed us to see Paul. I remember the door opening from the burn unit into the waiting area. It was not a doctor coming to talk with us and update us on Paul's condition. It was not even a nurse to prepare us for what we were about to see. It was a male nurse who stood in the doorway and yelled to us that he was ready now, and we could see him if we wanted to. He did not usher us in to see him but turned and walked away in another direction. So, I gathered my wife and two sons together, and we entered the burn unit for the first time.

As we crossed through an open area toward the nurse's station to ask which cubical Paul was in, a security guard yelled, "Halt!" to us from a distance. "All four of you can't go in there together," he said. I identified ourselves and told him that we were the family of the firefighter just admitted. He replied, "I know who you are, but you still can't all go in at one time." I then told him that the doctor said we could all go in together for the first time. He said, "I don't care what the doctor said, the rules are only two visitors at a time, besides, this is not visiting hours." Joey spoke up and said, "Daddy, you and mother go in, Stevie and I will go back and wait." I took my wife by the hand, and we went to the little glass-wall cubical to which we were directed.

I have to tell you that we were not prepared for what we saw. Paul was wrapped in white bandages and looked like an Egyptian mummy. There were tubes, hoses, and lines going everywhere. Motors were humming; pumps were pumping, and he lay there perfectly still. The attending nurse stopped her activities and silently moved against the wall and looked at us. We spoke to Paul, and tried to get a response, but he never responded to us. I was puzzled that he made absolutely no movement at this time when I saw him sit upright on the gurney a short time before. We did not know and were not informed that he had been given the paralyzing agent Norcuron. Medical records indicated it had been administered to prevent him from fighting the respirator.

His head was completely covered with bandages, in his mouth was a large plastic device with a huge clear tube attached to a respirator beside his bed. This was more than my wife could handle, and she began to sink toward the floor. I tried to catch her and support her, but she continued to grow limp. Soon she was complete dead weight; I struggled trying to get her out of the unit and back to the waiting area. The nurse never offered to help me with her at all. My wife is not a large woman, but when she became almost complete dead weight, it was hard for me to get her out of there by myself. I struggled and pulled and finally got her to the door, at which time some of the people in the waiting area helped me get her seated in a chair.

It fell on me to call our families back in our respective hometowns and our daughter in school. I had a very hard time with each call, but the hardest of all was when I had to tell Dawn that her brother was seriously injured. Paul and Dawn were only 18 months apart. They grew up playing together, attending school together, socializing together, singing together in church, and formed a bond that was remarkable. They shared things with each other that no one else knew. Though he had not talked very much about it, I knew Paul missed his sister very much while she was away at school. He talked with her by telephone as often as he could. He loved her very much. This call was hard to make. Lee College, now Lee University, is in Eastern Standard Time, and we were in Central Standard Time. It was already past noon there when I called. I told her about the fire that morning, and that Paul had been burned. Her first words to me were "Is he dead?" It was as if she knew immediately how serious it was. I told her he was still alive, but she needed to come home as soon as possible. It just so happened they were completing the first semester for the year at Lee, and she would be able to come home without much difficulty.

Clyde Roberts, a fine Christian man in our church who owned a flying service operating out of the Greenville Airport, came to me and offered to go get Dawn in one of his airplanes. We were most grateful. So, he flew his twin engine Aztec to Cleveland, Tennessee, and back in a very short time, bringing Dawn to us safe and sound. When she arrived at the hospital, we could see that she was very hurt and deeply concerned for her brother. She wanted to see him as soon as she could.

As my family began to arrive at the hospital in Greenville, it was very important for them to see Paul. The burn unit had set visiting hours during which only two visitors at a time were allowed to visit a patient. The total visiting time was about 10 or 15 minutes. In order for more than two people to visit a patient, it was necessary for visitors to spend only a few minutes and come out, which allowed two more to be able to visit. We would do this until the amount of visiting time had expired, then wait until the next visiting time.

During one visiting period, my sister Pam, took our youngest son, Stevie, age 11, into the unit to visit Paul. Stevie had not seen Paul, because he and Joey were ordered to leave the unit by a security guard earlier. He had something important that he wanted to tell his older brother. As he was speaking to Paul, a nurse interrupted him and told him that he was too young to be in the unit and he would have to leave. She was going to make him leave when my sister spoke up and said, "Just give us a minute, he has something he wants to say to his brother." After Pam spoke up, the nurse reluctantly allowed him to remain for another minute or two.

During the day, firefighters brought in coolers filled with ice and cold drinks, bags of chips, cookies, and food, even thermos bottles of hot coffee. I never touched any of the food or drinks, I had no appetite, but it was there for me if I wanted it. I appreciated the thoughtfulness of the firefighters. The day wore on, and soon people began to leave and the crowd became smaller. Late into the night, once again, it was just our little family left. I told my wife to take the children home and try to get some rest. I was going stay at the hospital and let them know if anything changed. She was extremely exhausted and needed rest so much that she reluctantly agreed. I remained at the hospital alone. It would have been a comfort to have had a member of the Fire Department with me that first night, but there was no one.

Through the long cold night, I tried to sit, but the chairs were so uncomfortable that I could not rest in them, so I walked the floor. I tried to pray, but it seemed as if every word I spoke came right back and hit me in the face. I went outside into the cold night air and looked up into the heavens. I literally begged God to let Paul live. He meant so much to me, I did not think I could live without him. I reminded God of my service to Him—leaving my family and friends and going wherever He wanted me to go and preach. Did not that count for something? I did not have anything to speak of materially. After 25 years in the ministry, all I had was my family. I prayed throughout the long hard night, "Please, God, do not take Paul from us." When the morning came, I was tired and exhausted. I had been up since early Sunday morning and had gone through the most demanding day of my entire life. My eyes were red and swollen from loss of sleep and crying. I needed a good dose of compassion and kindness right then, I needed it more than I ever needed it in my life.

It was around eight o'clock the next morning, Monday, December 4, I was still alone in the waiting area when the double doors leading into the burn unit swung open wide. It was not the doctor coming to give me an update on Paul's condition or explain his chances of survival. It was not a nurse coming to give me news of how well he made it during the night. It was not even a member of the hospital staff coming to see how things were with me or if I needed anything. Who was it? It was the chief of the hospital security. He walked into the room, looked all around, and then he looked at me. He did not ask me about my son, he did not even say, "I am truly sorry about the accident." In fact, he did not even say good morning. He said, "You're going to have to get this stuff out of here." He was referring to the ice chest, bags of food, and thermos bottles brought in by the firefighters. I just looked back at him; I was so stunned, I did not even respond. Looking directly at me he said, "I'm talking to you!" Now, I may not be the most intelligent person on earth, but since I was the only one in the room at that time, I knew he was talking to me. I told him that I did not bring the stuff in there that the firefighters did. He said, "I know who brought it in, but it was brought in for you, and you are going to have to get it out of here now." I was not feeling the best in my life right then; I had been up all day and all night. I walked the floor through the night and worried about my son and my nerves were on edge. Right then I was not in the mood for some jerk to come in early in the morning and order me to remove items from his rinky-dink hospital. Stuff that I had not brought in and had not requested that it be brought in. So I responded to him, "Sir, I've been up over 24 long, hard hours, and I've told you I didn't bring this stuff in here. I have a son back there in the burn unit that is fighting for his life, and I don't know if he is going to live or die. Right now I've got a lot more important things on my mind than this stuff in this waiting area. It's not bothering me, so if you want it out of here, you take it out, because I'm not touching it!" With that he turned around and went out the door into the hallway toward the administrator's office.

I stood there in dumb silence for a few moments, then I thought, *I don't know why this hospital is treating us like they are, but I going to speak with the administrator.* To this very day, I have no idea why our family was treated the way we were. We never asked for special treatment from anyone. However, in most cases when a public safety officer is injured or killed, the city, the hospital, and everyone involved offer exceptional kind and sympathetic care to the family. That was not the case with our family at all.

I immediately made my way to the office of the administrator. A young lady asked me if she could help me. I told her I wanted to see the administrator. She replied, "He has someone with him right now." As I looked toward his office, the door was standing about halfway open. I could then see who his visitor was. It was the chief of hospital security! I told the secretary, "That is the man I want to see him about." When I said that, the security chief got up from his seat and walked out, passing me without saying a word.

I spoke to the administrator only about the incident that had just occurred with the chief. He gave me a lot of double talk and got me out of his office as soon as he could, and he never did anything about anything.

Chapter 7

Five Days at the Mississippi Firefighters Memorial Burn Center

Our next five days were spent waiting at the hospital. We wanted to be as close to Paul as we could, night and day. During that time, family members from out of town arrived to be with us at the hospital. Their presence was a source of strength for us. I learned a powerful truth through that experience that I have tried to apply as circumstances present themselves. Your presence means more to a family in such a time than you could ever know. You do not have to say anything, just be there for the family. They will draw strength from your presence.

The burn unit waiting area was not comfortably furnished. There were no reclining chairs and no couches. It was furnished with straight chairs with little padding, which made resting very difficult. At night we would bring in air mattresses to sleep on, deflate them the next morning, and put them away until the next night. We would go home briefly to take a shower, change clothes, and then return immediately to the hospital. We remained as close to Paul as we possibly could day and night.

The burn unit had two doctors on staff. The directing physician also operated a cancer clinic located near the hospital where he spent most of his time.

The other doctor was the only plastic surgeon in town. Each time either of them came into the unit we were there. We questioned them repeatedly about Paul's condition. We were hoping for any tiny bit of improvement, some ray of hope. We just wanted them to give us some good news, tell us something positive, and help us feel better about Paul. We became puzzled when it appeared that we were getting conflicting reports from the two doctors. One doctor would tell us one thing and the other would tell us something altogether different. This confused us and made us very concerned about the quality of care Paul was receiving and of his chances for survival.

Immediately after learning of Paul's accident, Dr. Don Jenkins, Church of God State Superintendent of Mississippi came to the hospital. He was very supportive and assisted in my effort to gain information from the doctor. He understood I was in shock and unable to get a total grasp of the situation. He continually pressed the doctor about the possibility of transferring Paul to another facility, possibly a Shriner's hospital. I remember the doctor telling us if Paul lived long enough, there may be a chance for a lung transplant. I did not understand why he was talking about a lung transplant because I did not know the extent of his injuries.

A great concern of mine was his physical appearance. What would he look like after this was over? Would he be badly scared or what? Paul was not a vain person, but he did care about his appearance. He wanted to look his best at all times. His clothes had to be clean, neatly pressed, and perfectly matched. He wanted his hair to be neat and trim. His shoes had to be shined. He took great care to look his best anytime he was in public.

The surgeon assured us that he would be able to restore Paul's appearance to near perfect condition. We trusted him and his assurance relieved our concern. Of the two doctors, the surgeon was the one who appeared the most optimistic and encouraged us. However, in doing so, he gave us false hope. I do not know if he did it to make us feel better, or if he did not expect Paul to live; therefore, he would never have to validate his words. We are not sure what prompted his comments to us. But I learned later that it would have been virtually impossible for any surgeon to restore Paul to his natural appearance.

On one occasion, the surgeon allowed me to see Paul with the bandages removed from his badly burned face. It was very difficult for me to look at him in that condition. The surface tissue of his face was turning a pale gray color, highlighted with several dark spots scattered about. Beneath all the dead and dying tissue, I could see small clusters of exposed blood vessels, raw and bleeding. I wondered just how painful it was to him. I stood there looking at him and thinking of the few times that I had experienced a burn. I remembered how painful even the smallest burn was for me, and I could only imagine what it must have been like for him. It hurt me so much to see my son in that condition. Yet as painful as it was, I wanted to see him. I had to see for myself how badly he was injured.

After I saw him, I thought his mother might want to see him also. At first she rejected the idea completely, then reluctantly she decided that she really did want to see him. I knew it would be painful for her, but I thought she should see him if she wanted to. Paul was her son also, her own flesh and blood, and just like it was with me, there was something inside her that compelled her to see him. My heart went out to her, because I knew how she felt. She was the one person on earth who shared exactly the same feelings I had about Paul.

The surgeon explained to us that he would remove skin from Paul's back, hips, and legs to graft over the burned areas. He referred to it as harvesting the skin. His description of the procedure sounded very painful, but it was something that had to be done. He also informed us that he would probably remove his ears and plant them inside the walls of his stomach, reattaching them to his head at a later time. That information was very difficult for us to handle. But we realized we had to brace ourselves if we wanted to know the truth.

As the days passed, there did not appear to be any positive changes in Paul's condition. It was almost as if we were in a holding pattern just waiting for the inevitable. It was at that time I became very concerned about the care he was receiving and began to seriously consider transferring him to another hospital. The more I pondered the possibility, the more convinced I became that it should be done.

When I spoke to the doctor in charge about that possibility, he became very upset at the suggestion. He said he could do as much for Paul in Greenville as could be done for him in any other hospital. I then insisted he be transferred to another hospital. It was then the doctor told me if I made the decision to transfer him from Greenville, he would refuse to have anything more to do with his case. In light of all this, I made the decision to move him, because I honestly believed it was the best thing for Paul. I believed it then, and I still believe it now.

Because I had pastored a church in the St. Louis area for almost nine years, I had become very familiar with a number of fine hospitals in that city. One particular hospital had a well-known burn unit that was rapidly gaining recognition. I had visited it before and was very impressed by what I saw. I thought about moving Paul to that hospital if possible. When friends in St. Louis flew down to Greenville to see Paul, they also encouraged me to transfer him to St. Louis.

Because the doctor would not assist me in the transfer, I had to do it myself. I made a call on my own to St. John's Mercy Medical Center Burn Unit. I spoke with the directing physician and told him our situation. He informed me that it was their policy to accept patients only by referrals from other doctors or hospitals. When I informed him the doctor in Greenville said he that would not transfer him, he said, "Let me call that hospital, and I will call you back."

A few hours later, he called back and said he had spoken with the hospital in Greenville. He then said he was going to break with hospital policy and do something that was highly irregular. Based on information he had received from the hospital and from what I had told him, he would accept Paul as a patient. I was so relieved when he told me that I almost cried. He then told me Paul would have to be transported by air, that he could not possibly be moved by ambulance.

When St. John's agreed to accept him, I then had the responsibility of arranging for his transportation. I knew nothing about transporting critical care patients. I had absolutely no knowledge of medical air transportation and all the requirements and procedures involved. I began to inquire from any and every available source. It became an overwhelming ordeal for me until a kind, caring, hospital social worker offered to help. She was most helpful, and I shall always be grateful for her assistance.

Transporting him required a special critical-care transport team. We were able to make arrangements with the University of Alabama School of Medicine in Birmingham for the transfer. The cost to transport him would be almost $10,000. I did not have $10,000 at the time. Chief Frankie Williamson offered a line of credit on his house to guarantee the money needed for the transfer. We did not have to resort to doing that, but I will always be grateful to him for his willingness to do it. A member of the church put up the money needed, and we proceeded with the transportation without delay. The church member was repaid from a special fund that was set up at one of the local banks. Many people in the community responded and donated money to help. Troy McGaugh, who did not even know Paul, was moved with a heart of compassion and contributed $500. We shall always be grateful to him and the many other contributors who helped us in that time of need.

The transport team was great in working with us, and soon the arrangements were completed with both the St. Louis hospital and the Greenville hospital. Everything was now ready, and the transfer was scheduled for Friday, December 8. However, an ice storm hit and virtually paralyzed most of the Deep South, which caused the transfer to be delayed an extra day. As far as we were concerned, every hour was critical, and we could not get him moved soon enough.

When the Citation jet finally touched down in Greenville on that bitterly cold Saturday morning, it was a welcome sight indeed. The transport team immediately began the difficult task of transporting a critically injured patient from a hospital in one state to a hospital in another state. The special team consisted of a medical doctor, a registered nurse, a respiratory therapist, a pilot, and a copilot. Arrangements had been made in advance with the local ambulance service to provide transportation from the hospital to the airport.

Upon arriving at the hospital, they immediately took charge of the patient. Medical charts were quickly reviewed, up-to-the-minute stats and vital signs were obtained. Then quickly removing him from hospital life-support equipment, they connected him to their own. A lot of things were happening in that room in a very short time. It was obvious this group was very professional, and that gave us a feeling of confidence. They told us if it became necessary, they could perform in-flight surgery. That was reassuring, but we hoped it would not become necessary. Thankfully, it was not necessary.

Ironically, Paul had recently purchased a very nice Crimson Tide sweat suit with the University of Alabama logo on it. His sister Dawn was wearing it when the medical team arrived, it caught their eye, and they made a specific comment about it.

It should be understood that Paul was an Alabama football fan. He was also a Mississippi State, Ole Miss and Southern Mississippi fan. He really loved SEC football. Even though Southern Mississippi was not a member of the SEC, he loved their football, especially Reggie Collier and Brett Farve. I thought he would be pleased to know the University of Alabama medical team was transferring him to St. Louis. So, right there before everyone, I stood over him and told him, not knowing if he heard me or not.

Once they were ready to move Paul from the hospital, they placed him atop a gurney and rolled him outside to the waiting ambulance. He looked pitiful and helpless lying there on the stretcher connected to life support. His head and face were all bandaged, with plastic lines and tubes going in every direction. As they positioned him to be placed inside the ambulance, I reached down to give a hand in lifting him when someone tapped me on the shoulder. I looked around; it was the fire chief. He said, "Let me do that." I released the handle and backed away and watched them place Paul inside, close the doors and rapidly drive away.

Our family followed the ambulance to the airport and watched as they placed him on board the airplane. I asked if I could ride with him on the plane, but I was told there was no available space. Soon the cabin doors were closed, and they taxied into position for takeoff. Moments later the sleek jet went roaring down the runway like an arrow shot from the bow of the mightiest archer. Lifting itself majestically into the sky, it made a half circle over the city then set its course for St. Louis. I watched as the plane disappeared into the Delta sky, and I thought, *Paul, you get to fly once again.* That was something that he really loved to do. But his greatest flight was still to come!

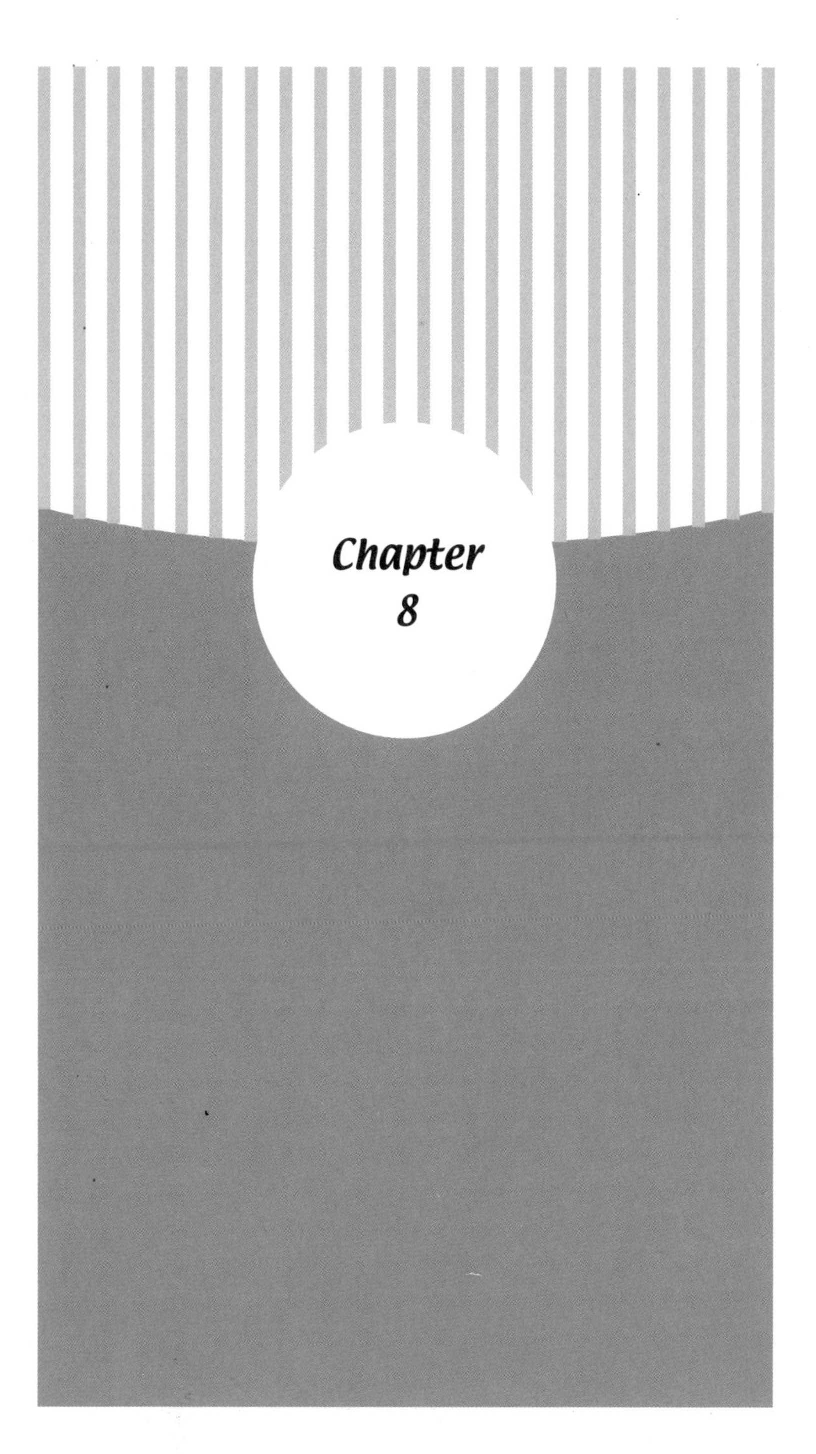

Chapter 8

The St. Louis Experience

As the jet carrying Paul began winging its way toward St. Louis, our family loaded into automobiles and began the journey to join him as quickly as we could. The trip would require approximately eight hours of hard driving.

I was already exhausted from losing sleep and rest at the hospital the past six days, so after driving for a short time, I became so sleepy that it was dangerous for me to continue. My wife then took over the driving, and I tried to rest, but it was difficult. Even though my body ached with exhaustion, my mind would not release my deep concern for Paul. As we drove through the long, cold night, I could hear Frances praying for Paul. Some of the things she said as she prayed broke my heart and brought tears to my eyes. I never spoke, I just listened, I guess she thought I was asleep.

We arrived at St. John's Mercy Medical Center around two o'clock in the morning. We were directed to the emergency area where we were given a brief update on Paul's condition and I was asked to sign necessary admission papers. We learned that he made the trip without incident. The doctors had completed their initial examination, and admitted Paul to the burn unit. The admitting doctor had left for the night, but we were told he would meet with us in the morning. We were then directed to the hospital critical care waiting area.

As the elevator came to a stop and the doors slowly opened, we saw four familiar faces standing before us. Waiting for us at that hour of the night were David and Laura Martin and Gordon and Bonnie Walker, two couples we had pastored during our time in St. Louis. We did not know they knew anything about Paul's injury. We certainly did not expect them to be waiting for us at the hospital at that time of the night, but there they were. They visited with us for about an hour before leaving. In our conversation with them, we were shocked to learn they knew things about Paul's injuries that we did not know. It bothered us that the doctors had not been completely candid with us about his condition.

We had our first consultation with the director of the burn unit early the next morning. He was very compassionate and soft-spoken. During our interview, he shared information with us that we had not been given prior to that time. He explained that Paul had third-degree burns over his head and face, both his hands were extensively burned, and he was severely burned in his lungs.

The director continued, telling us that Paul had the worst head injury that he had seen in his many years of practicing medicine. I recall his look of concern as he spoke to us about Paul. He told us that Paul's eyes were opaque. I asked, "Are you telling us that he is blind?" With a gentle nod of his head he said, "Yes." Then he added almost as if in unbelief, "You didn't know this either?" Recognizing we were struggling with this new information, he abruptly concluded the consultation. As he closed, he said softly that he had given us enough information for that time. He assured us he would continue updating us daily.

Over the next several days, we experienced roller-coaster emotions. We were certainly more optimistic now with him in the larger medical center. But we had to deal with the fact that his injuries were much more serious than we had believed.

Again, our little family huddled together and tried to comfort each other during a very difficult time. We tried to come to grips with the severity of his condition, as well as to be honest with ourselves about his chances for survival. We tried to muster faith and believe that even though it was a bad situation, God would help him. There was no attempt on our part to be super spiritual; we were simply reaching out with desperate faith. Each of us reached deep within and tried very hard to believe that he would survive. We all knew it would be very difficult, but we had to believe; we had to hold on for Paul.

I began reflecting back over the years how that I had preached faith in God for every situation we face in life. As an evangelist and a pastor, I had prayed for many people and had little difficulty in believing for their needs. Now that I needed a genuine miracle in my own family, it was difficult to have strong positive faith. But we did not stop hoping; we did not stop praying.

As our family sat together that first morning in the St. Louis hospital, two gentlemen came into the rather large waiting area. After looking around the huge room, they walked straight to us. They asked, "Are you the Smith family from Mississippi?" "Yes, we are," I replied. They informed us they were members of the Creve Coeur, Missouri Fire Department. St. John's Mercy Hospital is located in their fire protection district. "We've been told one of our brothers has been brought to this hospital. We've come to see about him," they said. "We've come to see what we can do for him, and what we can do for you." To say that we were surprised would definitely be an understatement. We were not expecting anything like that at all. We had never seen any of them before, and when they said, "One of our brothers has been brought to this hospital," it touched me very deeply.

I thanked them for coming, and I gave them a report of Paul's condition, as I knew it. But I stopped there. I did not ask them for anything. At that moment, I knew of nothing they could do, and neither did I feel they had an obligation. Those people did not know us, neither did they know Paul. I thought they were simply strangers trying to be nice. I must tell you I did not understand the camaraderie that exists within the fire services. I did not understand the brotherhood and concern they have for each other. As far as I was concerned, they had absolutely no obligations to Paul or to us. That is not to say that their offer was not appreciated, for it was.

After a brief visit, they handed me their calling card. "Please call us if there is anything we can do for Paul or for you," they insisted as they left. They told us, "We will be back to see about him." I honestly did not know if we would ever see them again.

I soon would learn the fire service has a creed: "We take care of our own." That creed is more than just words. It is a fact! It is a way of life with firefighters. They live by that creed. Before the day was over, those same firefighters returned. "How is Paul?" "Are there any changes?" "Can we do anything?" they asked. Then they said, "We know you will want to stay close to the hospital. We want you to know that you and your family have two rooms at the nearby Westport Plaza Holiday Inn. The charge for these rooms has already been taken care of. They will not cost you anything. They are for your family to use for as long as you need them." That blew our minds! We could not believe what we were hearing. We used these rooms to shower and change clothes. Then we would return to the hospital as soon as we could. The rooms were ours for the entire time Paul was in the hospital.

They did not stop there. He said, "We have made arrangements with Jonathan's Restaurant, here in the hospital, for your family to have your meals with them. Just go in anytime and have anything on the menu you desire, and it's all taken care of. If you have visitors with you at mealtime, please take them with you as well. Now, is there anything else you need that we can do?" We were absolutely speechless; that was more than we could comprehend. We had never experienced anything like that before.

Every day Paul was a patient at St. John's Mercy, one or two members of the Creve Coeur Fire Department came to the hospital to visit. They wanted to know Paul's condition and how we were doing; they did their best to make sure we lacked for nothing. After his death, several members of the department flew to Greenville to attend his funeral. I am sorry to say that I did not know they were at the funeral until several days afterward. If I had known they were there, I would have asked them to be honorary pallbearers.

The Creve Coeur Fire Department will always hold a very special place in our hearts for their kindness and support. They will never know just how much they helped and how much they will forever mean to the Smith family. They made a very difficult time much more bearable for us.

I had often wondered how the Creve Coeur Department was informed of Paul's transfer from Greenville to St John's. I always assumed someone from the Greenville Fire Department had informed them. Several years passed before I learned from Creve Coeur Chief William Brandes that St John's Hospital informed them.

Paul was in St. John's Burn Unit from December 9 to December 25. During those 17 days, we must have gone through every agony and emotion known to man. There were times when we were very optimistic and encouraged, then there were the times when we were very low and discouraged. All the stress and worry began to affect each of us, but we kept fighting because we knew Paul was fighting also.

I could not begin to tell you how many telephone calls we received during Paul's hospitalization. There were about five or six pay phones in the waiting area. Many times each member of our family would be on a phone and someone would answer another phone and call out, "Smith family!" We appreciated every call, but after answering so many calls, we got weary. Giving each caller an update on Paul's condition became a draining experience on us. Almost every caller wanted to know the details of the accident. They wanted to know if he was conscious or if he could say anything. Was he going to live? Would he look all right? I got the impression that each person thought he was the only one who had called and asked all those questions. It became very painful for each of us to give reports and details, regardless of who the caller was.

We got our rest at night by sleeping on one of the couches, if we were lucky, or in a nice recliner that was in the waiting area. We ate our meals in the very nice restaurant in the hospital. There were many times, however, when we just did not have an appetite, and we did not eat. The management of Jonathan's Restaurant was very gracious; they went out of their way to do anything they could for us. It was an unbelievable experience for us.

The hospital staff could not have been more accommodating. Every nurse, every technician, every physician was kind and considerate. I remember an emergency room physician coming to the burn unit and looking for us because she had heard about Paul. That doctor wanted us to know she was thinking about us and praying for Paul. I shall never forget the kindness of the wonderful Sisters of that fine hospital. They did everything they could for us. One of the Sisters came to me and said, "I know you have been sleeping in those chairs every night, and you can't get good rest that way. There is a bed in the dialysis treatment area located beside the burn unit. That bed is not used at night. I have made arrangements for you to sleep there and be close to your son. The bed will be changed with new linen each evening just for you. That will be your bed." I did not sleep in the bed, but I was deeply touched by her concern for me. Things similar to that continued to happen throughout our entire stay. I am not Catholic, but it made absolutely no difference with the Sisters of Mercy at St. John's Hospital. They gave our family as much attention and concern as they would have given the most devout Catholic family. I was surprised but very appreciative for all their kindness. I cannot thank them enough for the wonderful care they gave Paul and my family during the entire time we were there.

One very cold and snowy night, there was about six inches of snow and ice covering the ground.

The temperature was very low, and it was bitterly cold. Our family was huddled together in the hospital trying hard to keep our faith high and encourage each other. Things looked bad for Paul about then, and we were sinking in our spirits. We needed something at that moment to give us a new lift.

In the distance, I heard what appeared to be the sound of the diesel engine of a tour bus. Slowly, it came closer and closer to the hospital, my attention was fixed on the sound, and I thought, *That can't be Danny Murray and New Harvest.* New Harvest was a gospel music group based in Cleveland, Tennessee, made up of very talented Christian young people. Paul had been a member of the group as their bass player. His time with New Harvest was something that gave him personal fulfillment. He bonded with each member of the group in a special way. The only reason he left the group was his strong desire to return to the Fire Department in Greenville.

To our great surprise and delight, it was Danny Murray and New Harvest! There they were right there in St. Louis—all the way from Cleveland, Tennessee, and on such a cold night. We were so overjoyed as they came into the hospital that we all hugged and cried. It was very obvious to us that the group loved Paul, and we knew that Paul loved each of them.

After our family visited with them, they wanted to see Paul. I shall never forget the experience as the group gathered around his bed. Each member looked at Paul as he lay there dressed in bandages that completely covered his head and face. Each of their faces told a story as they fought back tears. They could hardly believe they were looking at the same young man who had traveled and sung with them only a short time before. The same person who had been so full of life and vitality now lay before them unable to lift a hand or acknowledge their presence.

For a few minutes, they gazed at Paul in stunned silence. Then Danny began to sing very softly. Judy Jacobs quickly joined in and began to sing along with him. Then another joined in, and one by one they all began to sing. Their voices blended together like the voices of angels. The nurses stopped their activities and listened, some of the nuns gathered just outside his room and stood listening to the beautiful singing, wiping occasional tears from their eyes. I do not know if Paul actually heard them or not, but I want to believe that he did. But that time was very special for us, and I believe it was special for Paul as well. Just knowing that his musician friends cared enough to come to sing to him and pray for him meant so much to each of our family. I do not know if anything like that had ever happened in that burn unit before or not, but I can tell you it was really something very special!

As the days passed, Paul continued to cling to life, even if only by the thinnest of threads. The doctors did everything they could for him, but his condition progressively worsened. He was given extremely high dosages of antibiotics. One doctor told me, "We are hitting him with everything we can."

With our approval, they even administered an experimental drug, hoping for success. The medical team also reached out to the St. Louis Medical Community for consultation on Paul's case. One hospital physician stated that more doctors had seen Paul than any other patient he knew. We are confident the doctors left no stone unturned in their efforts to save him. As the doctors fought for his life, we can only imagine how he must have also fought to live. But fight as he would, there was simply too much against him.

When it became necessary for him to go on dialysis, we were warned the treatment would place great stress on his already weak and exhausted body. The first treatment resulted in the removal of a large quantity of fluid. Immediately, we could see the results in his appearance, and we felt good about it. However, the very next dialysis treatment had to be aborted because of the stress it placed on his heart. His condition steadily declined after that.

The days passed, and we continued our vigil. It was now Christmas Eve. It really did not feel like Christmas Eve to me, but I knew it was. There was no joy or holiday cheer for the Smith family as we waited and hoped. For the first time I could remember there would be no last-minute Christmas shopping or rushing to buy that one last present. The ritual of my family getting together to celebrate by exchanging gifts and shooting fireworks would go on without us on this Christmas Eve. This Christmas Eve, we would continue as we had been for the last 21 days: sitting, waiting, and praying for a miracle—a Christmas miracle!

We waited in the harsh atmosphere of loneliness, sadness, and despair. We tried hard to find something to smile about. But our smiles had given way to the cruel reality that this might well be the last Christmas Eve we would have Paul with us. Barbara Keane came to the hospital with Christmas gifts for each member of our family. She knew we had not given any time or thought to gifts; however, it was Christmas Eve, and she made sure we each had presents. It was a very nice and thoughtful deed on her part, and it did lift our spirits and brought us a measure of Christmas cheer.

Joey and I were standing outside the burn unit doors when a nurse walked out and passed by us with a telling glance. She walked several steps down the hall before she turned and walked back to me. "I don't know what kind of church you people attend, or what you believe," she said. "But my church believes in divine healing, and I've put Paul on the church prayer list, and a lot of people are praying for him," she continued. I later learned that she was a member of a very large Charismatic church in St. Louis. Looking right into my eyes, she said: "I've been back there, and something is happening right now. And I believe Paul will have something to say as to what the outcome of this will be." I never had time to respond before she turned and walked very briskly down the hall. But to know that many more people were joining in prayer for Paul made me feel deeply grateful.

Late into the evening, Frances and Dawn decided to go to the hotel to freshen up. Joey and I remained at the hospital with Paul. Stevie was with the Keane family in Webster Groves at that time. As we were waiting, a male nurse from the unit came to me and said, "I just left the unit, something's going on back there, you may want to go see." Joey and I immediately went back to the unit.

As we entered his room, we saw the air mattress had been deflated and Paul was lying much lower on the bed than usual. He had been coded; the doctors and nurses had administered CPR and other life-saving techniques to revive him. Most of the IVs and life-supporting apparatus had been removed; however, the respirator and heart monitor were still attached. He was hardly breathing. His breaths were very weak and far apart. His body would give a slight quiver at times. The doctor said to me, "If something drastic doesn't happen within the next 15 minutes, it will be over!" It appeared that Paul was dying. As tears filled my eyes, I found myself in the most horrible moment of my life. I was watching my precious son die, and I could not do anything for him. This young man I loved so much and would do anything for, was at death's door, and I could do nothing. I had never felt so helpless. It was more than I could bear.

His right arm and hand were exposed, and so I held his arm. I did not ask permission to pray, I just began to pray as I held his arm. I was not really aware of what Joey was doing until I began to hear him praying aloud for his brother. As I looked up, Joey was reaching over my shoulder with his hand on Paul's chest. He began to pray with such volume until I began to try to get him to be a little softer. He looked at me with a stern look and said, "Daddy, Paul's dying, we've got to pray for him to live." He was not ashamed or intimidated to pray out loud for his dying brother right there before doctors, nurses, or anyone. I will always admire him for that.

Within minutes, Paul began to breathe more normally, the haunting bleeps of the heart monitor began to get stronger and more rapid, his vital signs began to stabilize. We called his mother, and told them to get back to the hospital as quickly as they could. As they rushed back, Joey and I remained in the unit with Paul.

When his mother and sister arrived back at the hospital, they were very upset. We tried to comfort them by telling them Paul was doing better. As we began to move back to the waiting area, the nurse told me that we could go in to see him anytime and as many times as we wanted. We returned to the waiting area, but continued to keep a constant check on him. Paul continued to hold stable the rest of the night.

The next morning I began to have renewed faith and a brand new hope for him. He did so well through the night, they reduced his oxygen level, as well as some of his medication. We knew God had touched him and restored his life, and we felt positive he would continue to get better. Each time we visited him he appeared to us to be improving or at least holding his own. We began to feel better than we had felt in several days. I thought, *This is going to be a good Christmas after all.*

Chapter 9

Christmas Sorrow

It was now Christmas Day. No one ever looked forward to Christmas with greater excitement than Paul did. It was a special day for him. But this Christmas would be different. There would be no celebrating for our family, no exchanging of gifts, no Christmas dinner. Rather, it was just our family alone many miles from home. The loneliness was so heavy you could almost cut it with a knife. Yet no one complained, we just sat together and prayed. The morning passed, and some friends from the Webster Groves Church came to the hospital to be with us. Paul's closest friend, Jeff Keane, was there. It was obvious that Christmas was not the same for him either.

Christmas afternoon, we were again called to Paul's room. Hurriedly, we made our way to the unit. As we approached, the double doors leading into the unit swung open and the doctor walked out. He had a telling expression on his face; he did not have to say anything for us to know it was bad. "It's all over," he said as he shook his head sympathetically toward me.

As we entered the room, I saw the nurses who had been involved in the life-saving effort with Paul. They looked saddened and very tired. They are professionals; they face that almost every day, yet it was clear they were visibly shaken. Stepping away from his bed they lowered their heads and allowed us that time with Paul.

The ventilator had already been removed. Most of the tubes and lines were gone. The heart monitor was now silent, I looked up at the screen and observed the straight line that told the chilling truth. I took a deep breath as I fought back tears. A sheet covered him from his waistdown. He lay motionless on the bed. No one said anything, but I knew it was over. I looked at him and thought, *What a wonderful son you were Paul. You never caused us any problems your entire life.* I stood there with my heart breaking and I thought, *I have never told Paul that I was proud of him as a firefighter—something he wanted to be most all of his life, something that was very special to him, and I had not shared that part of his life with him as I should have.* Being a firefighter cost him his life, but he was doing what he wanted to do. It is a brave and honorable profession, and I was indeed truly proud of him. The entire family was proud of him, yet I had never told him so.

I walked to his bedside and put my arms around his still warm body. I spoke into his ear, "Paul, you are the finest son any father could hope to have. I love you so much, and I am so proud of you. And I am so proud of you as a firefighter. You are my hero!" I could feel someone tugging gently on my shirt, I thought, *They think I'm going to loose it!* Slowly, I arose and turned and walked out. Joey followed me outside Paul's room.

His mother remained in the waiting area for a few minutes, unable to find the strength to go into the unit. She knew within herself something very terrible was happening. A few minutes passed before she was able to go in and see her son. As she turned from the long hallway leading to the burn unit, she looked straight into his room. With that one look, she immediately knew Paul was dead. She cried out, "He's only 22 years old." Then she began to fall limp to the floor. A nurse who just happened to be pushing a wheelchair in the hall at that time was right behind her. As she began to collapse, the nurse pushed the wheelchair right under her and broke her fall. She sat down in the wheelchair and completely passed out.

Nurses worked with her, putting cold cloths on her face and smelling salts under her nose. As she regained her composure, she looked at me and we embraced. We cried as our broken hearts melted together in a chorus of deepest sorrow. I then fell limp across a bed that for some reason had been placed in the hallway. I did not pass out; I just became weak in body and did not have strength enough to stand. Some time passed before I regained my strength and stood to my feet. Nearby, Paul's closest friend Jeff fell to his knees and began to sob softly. I saw that several people from the Webster Groves church had arrived and were gathered in the hallway. They had interrupted the time with their families on Christmas Day to come to the hospital to be with us. Even though we did not get to talk much with them at the hospital, their faces are forever etched in our memories. They had shown that they cared. They were there. That was important to us!

Christmas was Paul's favorite time of the year, not because he gave or received an abundance of expensive gifts, but rather for what the Christmas season is all about. To him Christmas was an eternal fact, not simply a feeling. The Spirit of Christmas affected Paul in a most profound way; I have never seen anyone else as moved by Christmas as Paul was.

He looked forward to every Christmas with great anticipation. He was looking forward to Christmas 1989 in his usual excited manner. He wanted to maximize every moment of every day during the holidays. It was as if he inhaled the hustle and bustle of Christmas and became intoxicated by the stimulation of the holiday spirit. He enjoyed little things that many people overlook; each one became a moment of magnificence to him. He looked forward to his Mother's Christmas dinner, the exchanging of gifts with the family, and as always, he wished for snow.

To Paul, each gift he gave was special. With him, gifts were never just a quick "pick up," a "fast wrap," or a casual presentation to someone. Each gift had to convey a special feeling from his heart. As was his usual manner, he had his gift list for each member of the family long before the traditional Christmas shopping began. After his death, we found his Christmas gift list for 1989. He had something very nice and specific for each member of the family. He had selected a very nice Gerber hunting knife for me.

How very strange that he would die on Christmas Day! Christmas is a time for joy and happiness. It is not a time for dying. My first response was, "Why did Paul die on Christmas Day?" It seemed so wrong to me that Paul should die on the one day that meant so much to him. Why not New Year's Day? Why not his own birthday or some other holiday? Why did it have to be Christmas Day? I wrestled with this for 14 years before I realized that on Christmas Day, Paul received the greatest gift ever—his admission into heaven!

Chapter 10

The Afterglow

Immediately after Paul's death, I had to make several phone calls to various parties to inform them of his passing. I called the Greenville Fire Department who in turn notified the two local television stations. I called a member of the New Life Church of God in Greenville who immediately passed the information to the membership.

When I called my family in Poplarville, they had gathered for their traditional Christmas dinner at the home of a cousin. I was at the lowest level of my entire life. My world had just collapsed around me; my sun had suddenly stopped shining. It was a terrible experience. I thought, *How can they be eating Christmas dinner when my son has just died? Why wasn't any of my family here with us? I would have been with them if it had been their child dying,* I thought these things to myself, I did not even share them with my wife or children. Maybe I overreacted, but I almost felt as if I had no family. I must confess it took me some time to get over the pain and disappointment I experienced at that time.

I had to finally accept the fact that life goes on regardless of our circumstances. Other people do not put their lives on hold when our lives tumble into tragedy. They continue to live; they do not stop laughing; they do not stop living. I had to accept the fact that people will continue to eat, visit, and celebrate.

Life goes on as before. That is just the way it is. This was a very difficult learning experience for me.

Sid Keane, a family friend who was very close to our children, Paul and Dawn, came to the hospital immediately after Paul's death. He graciously offered the home of his daughter for our family and friends to gather for the night. His daughter and her family were out of town for the holidays. It was a very gracious offer and fit our needs perfectly at that time.

Shortly after leaving the hospital, we were joined by Charlie and Suzy Fowler, who had flown in from Panama City, Florida. Charlie is an evangelist we had known for many years. He is a man who is gifted with great faith in God. He has encountered many tragedies in his own life where faith in God was all that sustained him. He has had the misfortune of several airplane crashes. The most recent occurred when he experienced instrument failure as he attempted to land in severe weather in Panama City. That crash almost took his life, but he survived only by a miracle of God. At the time of Paul's death, Charlie had not yet fully recovered from that accident. He was still walking with crutches, and it was a real effort for him to move about.

Charlie and Suzy were very close to our children. Paul, Dawn, and Joey had sung for them in many of their revivals and at their school in Mountain View, Arkansas. Charlie would fly them from St. Louis to his school in Arkansas, and they dearly loved it. In fact, Paul would fly with Charlie anywhere at anytime.

It was only a few years earlier that Charlie's voice box had been crushed in another airplane crash in Illinois. After his release from the hospital and while still under the doctor's care, he attended a service at the church I was pastoring in St. Louis. He was unable to speak, and doctors said that he would never speak again. It was in that service that I witnessed God immediately restore his voice. So I knew Charlie Fowler had great faith. I had witnessed it in his life.

On the morning of December 25, we knew things were really bad and unless something happened very soon, Paul would not make it. It was then, at the last minute that I called Charlie at his home in Panama City, Florida. I interrupted his Christmas with his family and asked him to come to St. Louis and personally pray for Paul. I was aware that he could pray for Paul at his home in Florida. I also was aware that he had been praying for him. But I had a very strong impression that if Charlie Fowler came to the hospital and laid his hands on Paul and prayed for him, Paul would live. I believed that God would honor the prayers of this man for Paul in the same manner He had honored his prayers for needs in his own life.

That wonderful man and dear friend immediately made arrangements to come to St Louis to pray for Paul. He and his wife, Suzy, took the first plane out of Panama City. They were still in flight, just at the outskirts of St. Louis, when Paul died. I have often wondered what would have happened if Charlie had made it to the hospital in time and prayed for Paul.

After their plane landed, the Fowlers immediately made their way to the hospital only to learn that Paul had died a short time before. They made inquiries and searched until they tracked us down at the home of our friends in Webster Groves. Charlie and Suzy stayed with us and gave us support through the night. They remained close by our side through the funerals and the interment. They still remain close to our hearts today.

I did not like the thought of Paul being left in the hospital morgue until after Christmas. But it was Christmas Day; the funeral homes were closed. It seemed as if we had no choice but to leave him at the hospital until Christmas had passed. I was so troubled by this that Sid Keane suggested that he contact his friend at Gerber Chapel in Webster Groves on our behalf. He talked with them and made arrangements for Paul to be moved from the hospital to the funeral home that day. That was done as a special favor for me, and I deeply appreciated it. I have been in hospital morgues, and I just did not want Paul to spend Christmas night in the morgue wrapped like a side of beef.

That night, phone calls began coming in from all over the country. I do not know how the news spread so quickly, especially on Christmas Day, but it did. I do not know how people got the phone number where we were staying, but they did. Friends, family, and ministers called to offer their sympathies. We were on the phone with people until late into the night.

Christmas night, 1989, was the longest and hardest night that I have ever experienced. I could not bear the thought of Paul being gone. I felt so alone, so helpless. I did not feel like I could live. I did not feel like I should live. What did I have to live for?

We spoke with the friends who were with us at the home. Someone made coffee. We walked from room to room until late into the night. When my wife and I finally tried to rest, we just could not. There was no sleep for either of us. Our bodies were tired and exhausted, but our minds raced nonstop until daybreak the next morning. I wanted so much to wake up and discover that it was all a bad dream, a terrible nightmare, that it really had not happened at all. I wanted things to be as they were before. I would have given everything I had if that could have happened.

The next morning, Mr. Keane took our family to the funeral home where we selected a beautiful oak casket and made arrangements for transporting Paul back to Mississippi. I had a picture of Paul with me for the morticians to use in their restorative work. Since Paul loved flying, I thought he would like being flown back home one last time. So, I arranged for Paul to be flown from St. Louis to Memphis. Mortermer Funeral Home would then transport him from Memphis to Greenville. White Funeral Home of Poplarville would join us for the Greenville funeral, and they would transport Paul to Poplarville for the second funeral and interment.

It was all pretty involved with three funeral homes and many details. However, thanks to some real professionals—Don Gerber, Don Mortimer, Johnny Smith, and Freddie White—it all came together and worked out very well.

Early Years

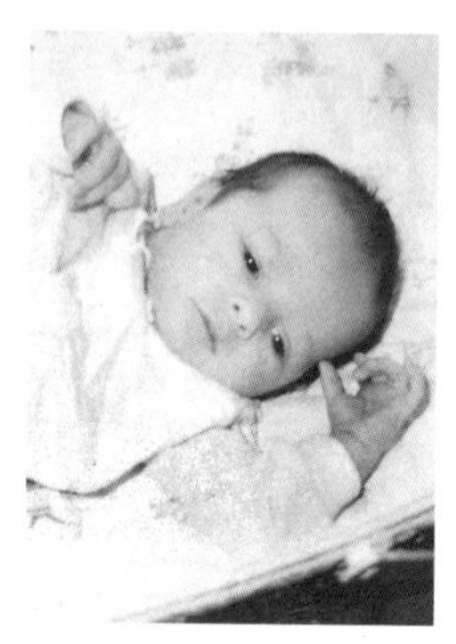

Teen Years

He was
a good guy!

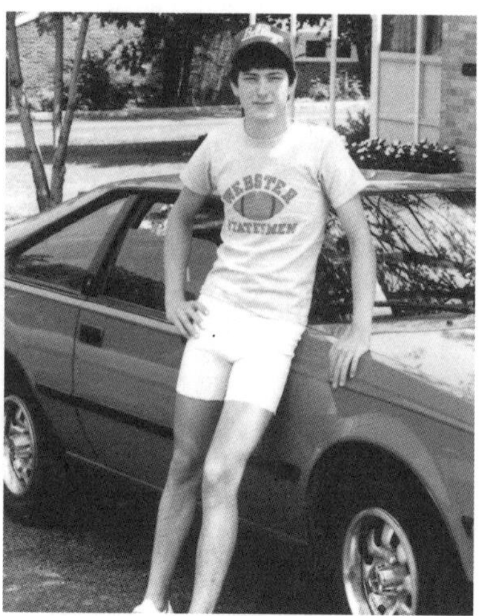

The Firefighter

The Memorial Service

December 1989

SUNDAY	MONDAY	TUESDAY	WEDNESDAY	THURSDAY	FRIDAY	SATURDAY
					1 Poplarville	2 Swap Poplarville
3 Poplarville	4 Poplarville	5 Come back work	6	7 Pearl Harbor Day, 1941	8 $!!	9
10	11	12	13	14	15	16
17	18	19	20	21 Winter Begins	22 $	23 Chanukah
24 / 31	25 Christmas Poplarville	26	27	28	29	30

This calendar, marked by Paul, shows his plans for December, 1989.

Chapter 11

We Say Good-Bye

The night of Paul's death was long and agonizing, and we barely closed our eyes. The next morning we made the trip to the funeral home to select his casket and make arrangements for his return to Mississippi. Soon after completing the arrangements, our family loaded into our automobiles and made the trip back home on December 26.

Charlie and Suzie Fowler rode with my wife and me in our automobile. It was good for us to have them along. So many things continued to bounce around in our heads as we struggled with his death. The Fowlers were sensitive to our grief and allowed us to withdraw into our own moments of pain and sorrow without comment or giving us pep talks.

Once we returned home, there was hardly any time for us to rest even though our bodies were tired beyond description. So many things had to be taken care of before the funeral. It may have been that our involvement with arrangements for the funeral and other affairs served to shield us from the devastating pain that we would have otherwise endured.

Planning Paul's funeral required meeting with church leaders and fire officials, selecting pallbearers, inviting singers, and selecting the speakers. It was all very stressful because we wanted to involve everyone we believed Paul would have wanted. At the same time, we did not want to overlook someone who should have been included. It was very important to me for Paul to have an appropriate, meaningful funeral. So I pushed myself; I worked long into the night preparing and working on details. I was physically and mentally exhausted, but I continued to plan the funeral to the best of my ability.

I was alone in my office when a knock came at the door. Dr. Travis Richardson, friend and family physician, entered. Dr. Richardson had taken a special interest in Paul and had helped him through some difficulties in his life. As he entered, he extended his sympathy, expressing his profound sorrow for our loss. Then he said something that I did not fully understand at the time. He said, "Bevon, you have to understand this was an accident. I don't care what anyone tries to tell you. Remember, this was an accident." I do not even remember responding to his remarks, but I have never forgotten them.

As time passed, I think I began to understand what he said. Too often we attempt to give an explanation to something when we have no explanation. We always search for the "why" behind everything that happens. We seem to believe that "Nothing can just happen, there has to be a reason behind everything," that there must always be "a divine signature on each and every thing we experience in life." Accidents do not just happen: "It is always God's will for this to happen, or for that to happen." In doing so, we often complicate, confuse, and give false meaning, even if it is well intended. I firmly believe God is always in control and nothing happens without His knowledge or consent. Yet, I do not accept the idea that God took my son. Paul was the victim of a needless accident that should never have happened. It was the negligence of man that took his life, not an act of God.

Because our hometown is in South Mississippi and we lived in North Mississippi, it was necessary to conduct two funeral services for Paul. The first service was held on Thursday, December 28 at the New Life Church of God in Greenville where I was pastor and Paul was a member. The second service was conducted Friday, December 29 in our hometown of Poplarville in South Mississippi where he was born and where he is buried.

Before the Greenville funeral, the fire chief informed me that they had never experienced a "line-of-duty" death in their department. Their department was not experienced in fire-funeral protocol; therefore, he was struggling to find a plan for the funeral. He asked me if there was anything I would like the department to do. He suggested several things, including placing Paul's casket on one of their new E-One fire engines. At that time, I did not know the significance of having his casket ride in procession atop the fire apparatus. That is a very special honor reserved for only firefighters killed in the line of duty. The chief did not share that information with me, and I declined his offer. If I had known the significance, I most definitely would have wanted him to be placed on the fire engine.

I did not understand that firefighters who die in the line of duty are honored with the United States Flag draped over their casket. The flag was presented to us but was not placed over his casket. I regret we did not have Taps played at the cemetery, as is the custom for firefighters killed in the line of duty. It was my understanding at the time that Taps were for military personnel only. Neither did I know bagpipes were a tradition for fire funerals, so bagpipes were not played either.

The chief appeared willing to do anything we wanted for the funeral; we just did not know what to ask for. Today, I could organize a very impressive fire funeral, but at that time, I was not equipped with the necessary information. At his invitation, I did make a couple of suggestions. At my request, a fire department honor guard was placed at Paul's casket around the clock for the Wednesday night visitation. Members of the Greenville Fire Department made up the honor guard and served as honorary pallbearers for both funerals.

Because music was so much a part of Paul's life, his funeral featured more than the usual amount. Singers that shared his love for music during his lifetime were there to provide a beautiful tribute. They included The Johnson Family, Lemuel Miller, Judy Jacobs, Danny Murray and New Harvest. A recording of Paul himself singing "I Don't Need To Know Tomorrow" was played during the service. A local television news anchor referred to that song as the most moving part of the funeral. His funeral became a celebration—a celebration of his life!

Dr. R. Lamar Vest, general overseer of the Church of God, delivered the funeral message in Greenville. Rev. Paul Henson, for whom Paul was named, brought the funeral message in Poplarville. Other ministers who spoke included Charlie Fowler, Dr. James Jenkins, Lemuel Miller, and Bennie Jones. Each speaker brought words of comfort and spoke of personal experiences they had shared with Paul.

Charlie Fowler, an evangelist who travels in his private, twin-engine airplane, told of Paul's great love of flying. Many times when flying together, he would allow Paul to sit at the controls and fly his plane, and how much Paul loved it. We knew this was true, because he never missed an opportunity to fly with Reverend Fowler or with Chris Roberts after we moved to Greenville. The Reverend Fowler concluded his remarks by saying, "Paul really loved to fly, and on Christmas Day, he took his greatest flight!"

I truly believe that Paul was honored with the most beautiful funeral service that I have ever witnessed. Both services impacted those in attendance in a very powerful way. Dr. Lamar Vest was so moved by the service that he spoke of Paul's funeral before over 18,000 people at the Church of God General Assembly the following August.

Overflow crowds gathered in both locations for the memorial services. Closed circuit television carried the services to those gathered in adjacent buildings. Fire officials from throughout the South attended both services and provided escort, honor guard, and a display of fire-fighting equipment.

On the night of his burial, a very heavy rain fell. It rained hard throughout the night, which only added to our already heavy sadness. Some of Paul's closest friends from St. Louis stayed with our family at our little country house located near the cemetery. We tried to comfort each other as we struggled through the long night.

I made the decision to remain near Paul's grave over the weekend. In my state of mind, I did not feel that I could fill my pulpit on Sunday. Our church understood this and graciously allowed us the time for ourselves. I knew that I had to return to the pulpit as soon as possible, but that Sunday was not the time.

Also, I needed strength and comfort greater than I had ever needed before. Growing up as a boy, I had spent a great deal of time in the woods near where Paul's freshly formed grave now is. Those same woods had served as a sanctuary for me during many heartaches and painful experiences of my younger years. When things overwhelmed me, I could go into those woods and feel safe and secure. I would always leave the woods feeling much better than I did when I entered them.

Once again, I returned to those same woods where the little creek flows lazily across the rocks and sand bottom, where beech trees line the creek banks, shutting out the heat from the sun with their massive canopies. This was the place of my youth, where I spent many hours watching the squirrels and the birds dash from tree to tree. This time, however, my visit was much different. This time I would leave with a heart filled with more pain than I had ever known. Even though I had often found solace among the trees, on that day the pain was greater than the sanctuary of nature could erase.

Our dear friend and mentor in the ministry, the Reverend M.H. Kennedy, filled the pulpit that Sunday while we remained in Poplarville. He was a wise and experienced man who ministered to the church with heartfelt compassion. His ministry was good for the church and helped prepare them for our return.

The church exhibited great compassion and wanted to shield our family from any worry or concern about the operation of the church. Laymen leadership stepped forward and guided the congregation with amazing skill. Friends in the ministry cancelled appointments to assist us in that time of need. They were more than willing to serve us in any way they could. It made me happy to be part of such a great church family.

Chapter 12

The Empty House

Paul was buried on Friday; I made the decision to remain in Poplarville over the weekend. A few days after the funeral a neighbor knocked at our door and told us of some firefighters visiting Paul's grave early that morning. I went to the cemetery as quickly as possible, but they had already departed. Placed at Paul's grave was a beautiful plaque honoring Paul, resting on a pair of firefighters boots, or turnouts as they are known. I was deeply touched by the action of those firefighters, even though their identity remains anonymous.

My family made the trip back to Greenville on Saturday; darkness had fallen before we arrived. As we entered our home for the first time after his funeral, we were overwhelmed with the heaviest spirit of sorrow I have ever experienced. We could hardly stand on our feet. It was extremely hard for us, knowing that Paul would never enter our home again. The experience was frightening. No one said anything to anyone; each of us toiled with the harshness of the moment, and each of us reacted in an individual manner.

We had barely walked inside when the phone rang. Reluctantly, I answered it. It was Robert Procter, a minister friend calling from Bakersfield, California. Bob and his family attended our church in St. Louis during the four years he served as State Youth and Christian Education director for the state of Missouri.

Bob was well acquainted with our family and knew Paul very well. He expressed his sympathy, explaining that he had tried repeatedly to reach us following Paul's death.

He began to tell me a most unusual story concerning Paul. He had been in contact with people who updated him on Paul's condition while he was in the hospital. On Christmas Day as his wife prepared their Christmas dinner, he went to a secluded place in his home and began to pray for Paul. In the course of his prayer, he prayed for each thing that he knew was wrong with him. He prayed for his severely burned face, his blinded eyes, his lungs and respiratory system, his failing kidneys, and unstable blood pressure.

He said, "As I prayed for each of Paul's needs, I suddenly began to have an experience such as I have never had in my life." He continued, "As I was praying, suddenly I saw Paul's hospital room with Paul on his bed. There appeared the brightest light I've ever seen. The brightness of that light filled that hospital room. Suddenly, Paul sat up in the bed, looking directly toward that very bright light. Paul had the most awesome expression on his face, as if he were looking at the most beautiful sight he had ever seen. That is when I noticed Paul's face was no longer burned. At that moment, he was completely whole and looked as he always looked. There were no burns, no scars, his eyes were wide open and seeing, and he was smiling a big smile." I began to weep as he told me this amazing story.

He continued, "As I watched, Paul was lifted from the bed and began to float toward the light. He floated right into the light and disappeared." Then he said, "I stopped praying and went to where my wife was preparing dinner." He said to her, "Linda, I just saw a vision of Paul. He will be either healed, or God will take him home today." Bob said to me, "Bevon, I had a vision of Paul leaving this world. I've never had a vision before in my life, but I had that one."

I have to be honest, I am more than a little skeptical of anyone who says they have visions, or that God speaks directly to them. When I hear someone say that, a red flag goes up automatically. But I know Bob Proctor. I know the kind of life he lives. I have confidence in what he says. He is not a showman or a con artist; he is a genuine Christian man who does not engage in idle talk. I believe him. There was no reason for him to tell me that story unless it was true.

I cannot explain why God allowed him to see that vision in California hundreds of miles from where Paul died in Missouri. But as a matter of fact, Missouri is in the Central time zone, California is in the Pacific time zone. Linda, Bob's wife, was preparing Christmas dinner, and Bob saw a vision after the noon hour in California. Paul died at 2:25 p.m. in Missouri. There is a two-hour difference in the time in Missouri and California. I believe Bob saw in a vision the very moment Paul left this life.

What a way for us to return home! Was it a confirmation that Paul was all right, or was it something else? His phone call came at a time when we needed something special. As we reflected on his story, each of us drew new hope and assurance that Paul was home now, and we did not have to worry about him anymore. I am sure there will be many who will be skeptical and totally discount this story. Believe what you will, it gave comfort to our family.

It was my desire to be back at our church the week following the funeral. However, being there did not mean that I could fill the pulpit. Our friend

Lemuel Miller flew in from Florida and ministered the second Sunday after Paul's funeral. Paul always appreciated Lemuel's musical talents, as well as his pulpit ministry. They were very good friends. It seemed appropriate to have Lemuel with us for the weekend. He not only ministered to the church; he ministered to our family as well.

I felt that I needed to speak in church the third weekend after the funeral. There were many who encouraged me to allow more time to pass before I attempted to go back to the pulpit, but I felt the need to return. The longer I delayed my return the more difficult it would become.

The church was filled to capacity for that Sunday service. The congregation was very sympathetic and kind toward us. I could recognize they felt our pain. I soon began to understand that our church family had suffered a loss also, and they were grieving with us. They loved Paul, and their hurt was deep.

Once we were back at home, we found almost everything was different. I felt so alone, so terribly lonesome. The loneliness had a frightening feel about it that is difficult to explain. There was a common feeling among us; none of us wanted to be alone. From the time Paul was injured until after the funeral, we had been surrounded by a lot of people. People from all walks of life, including the news media, were at the hospitals and at both funerals. For a full month there were many people around us every day, and suddenly there was no one. It was a strange and difficult adjustment for us to make.

A news reporter from one of the local television stations in Greenville came to our home and visited with my wife and me. She was not a Mississippi native and did not know Paul personally. However, she was so deeply touched by his death, especially his funeral, that she wanted to talk with us. In our conversation, I detected that she had interviewed other people who knew Paul. From her pursuit of the news story, she had concluded he was indeed a special person. She said she had even called her mother back home and discussed the funeral. She told her mother how much she was affected by Paul's recording that was played at his funeral. She wanted to know more about Paul, and we appreciated her visit.

In an effort to comfort others in their times of grief, people sometimes feel they must make comments. That is not always true; in fact, sometimes it would be more helpful to remain silent than to say things that have no meaning, or worse still, to offend the bereaved. For example, shortly after I returned to my office, a visitor came by. Feeling that he should say something beyond his expression of sympathy, his words staggered me.

He wanted me to know that he surely understood how I felt in the loss of my son. He related that his sister-in-law had a pet dog that recently died. She loved the dog so much and was so upset that they purchased a Rubbermaid container to be used as a coffin for the dog. They even had a little ceremony, and then buried the dog in a nice spot.

I was speechless. How could anyone equate the death of my son with the death of a dog? I did not need to hear someone compare my son's death to that of a poodle. Yet, he thought he understood my loss.

I do not have to tell you that I did not draw too much comfort from his visit. While many others simply came by, and by their coming, we knew they cared. I have forgotten most of the things said to me during that time, but I do not believe I have forgotten one person who came to visit us.

Paul had a beautiful liver-colored Labrador Retriever named Bruser. That dog loved Paul as much as any dog I have ever seen. After working out his shift, he would come home, go into the backyard, and play with that dog before he went inside the house. After Paul died, that dog was not the same. He appeared to be waiting and looking for Paul to come home every day. Within a few months, Bruser was dead. I believe he grieved himself to death over Paul. I buried the dog in the woods near Paul's grave in South Mississippi.

Chapter 13

Life Without Paul

Ruby Flannagin was an amazing woman in many ways. Losing two husbands and two sons in death, her strength, stamina, and tenacity were unparalleled. Looking directly into my eyes, she said, "When I lost my husband, it was as if someone cut off my right arm. I was greatly handicapped and couldn't do anything for myself." She continued, "But when I lost my son, it was as if someone cut my heart right out of my body."

Having never experienced the loss of a spouse, I can only imagine what that must be like. I can, however, identify with the "heart" emotion in losing a child. I can think of no better description for a bereaved parent than what Ruby said. Perhaps it is the most difficult experience any human can face in this life. I can think of nothing harder.

The tragedy is, most people never really know how much their children mean to them until they are gone. In the death of a child, a spouse, or a close loved one, we are eager to bestow accolades of praise and honor upon them. We recall the many things that made them special to us, yet they never hear one word we have to say about them. Why do we wait until they are dead before we express our love for them and declare what they meant to us? Why do we keep our love and affection securely guarded under lock and key? Why do we not share our affection with those we love? Why do we not give our loved ones our hugs, our smiles, and our flowers while they can still enjoy them? It would mean so much more if they heard us say those wonderful nice things about them while they are alive.

I always knew Paul was special, but I never realized how special, until after his death. He was a great asset to me personally; for example, he would mow the grass, shovel the snow, paint a building, and even entertain our guests. He was constantly doing things behind the scenes to lighten my work and make me look good. He always made sure the church sound system was working and set properly before every worship service. He would check the lighting, making sure it was working properly, even double-checking the temperature in the building to assure comfort. If I needed anything special for the day, he made sure I had it.

In addition to all the things he did behind the scenes, he made a great contribution to the worship service with his music. God really patted him on the back and blessed him with musical talent. He had the ability to play six different musical instruments. I could always count on him for a vocal solo or a duet with his sister. It is very obvious to me now that he contributed much more than I ever realized. I think what a great music director Paul would be today if he were alive. I just know he would be truly awesome.

It seems so unreal that one day I had the benefit of his talents and abilities, the next day I did not. One day life was good; the next day life suddenly lost its meaning. It was difficult to accept the fact that I would no longer have him or his tremendous talents to depend upon. It is very difficult to describe the emptiness that flooded me and the hopelessness I faced.

Immediately following his death, I lost the desire, the drive, or the heart to do practically anything. Nothing made any difference to me anymore. Any attempt I made at almost anything would soon prove to be much more difficult than before. My ability to concentrate was lost, to the point that no matter what I tried to do, my mind always drifted back to Paul. I was overwhelmed by his memories.

I found myself having night sweats. I would doze off to sleep only to suddenly awake with the most horrifying feeling I had ever experienced. Many times the episode resulted in my almost jumping completely out of bed. I would often awake, struggling for breath. I have actually had to dash outdoors in the middle of the night in order to breathe easier.

During that time, I lost my appetite for food. I did not want to go anywhere or be around anybody, especially if they were enjoying themselves. I felt guilty if I enjoyed anything the slightest little bit. I began to feel responsible for his death. I thought it must have been my fault. I should have been able to foresee the danger of fighting fires. I should have been able to protect him. I felt guilty that I was still alive. I did not feel I had the right to live and Paul be dead.

Strangely, during the time we spent at the hospitals, through the funerals, and afterwards, I had not actually shed very many tears. All the time I was hurting within, but tears were not falling from my eyes. It bothered me, and I wondered why I did not cry? Then one night it happened. Approximately three months after Paul's death as I prepared for bed,

I noticed a family picture my wife had placed on my nightstand. That particular picture was taken at a General Assembly a few years earlier. Taking a look at Paul in that picture, I was suddenly overcome by so much grief until I could hardly stand it. I began to cry, and immediately tears began to gush profusely. The experience was so excruciating, I thought I would surely die. I have never experienced such emotion. I continued to cry harder and harder into the night. My wife became concerned and attempted to help me stop crying. It was as if emotions had backed up within me, and suddenly it broke loose. It felt as if a dam broke within me releasing tons and tons of water with great force.

I was not the only member of the family who suffered. We all did in our own way. Many nights I listened to my wife sobbing in the darkness. When most everyone else was sleeping, she would spend the night crying with a broken heart. Of all the people in the world, she was the one who hurt just as much I did. I wanted to lighten her grief, but there was no way I could. We were on an agonizing journey, a journey of grieving. I soon discovered that unless one is on this journey, he simply cannot understand the trip.

One pitfall I caught myself falling into was that of being consumed with my grief, to the point of almost being selfish with it. I suddenly realized that our three other children were dealing with their loss and needed the support of their parents. It was almost as if they were competing with the ghost of their brother for our attention and affection. I am sure they felt shut out to a large degree, but they were kind and never made an issue of it. They continually heard us speaking about how great and wonderful Paul was, as if he had been perfect. They knew he had not been perfect; he had possessed imperfections just like everyone else. Perhaps they knew him better than his Mother and I knew him. They knew he was a flesh-and-blood human who made mistakes. Yet, they never challenged us or gave any indication that our fixed attention on his memory troubled them. When I came to understand this, I immediately reached out to them, and I have never been sorry.

While most of the people in my church continued to show compassion, there were some people who thought we should be over our grief within a few weeks. One member of our church staff remarked, "It's time for pastor to just let him be dead now." They did not understand the grief process and showed little compassion for us when we needed it most. Yes, he was dead; I had to let him be dead; there was not anything I could do; I had no choice.

With stubborn faith, I believed right up until his death that Paul would live and be all right. Some people said I was in denial. It was not denial; it was a combination of things. After he died, I struggled with my personal faith level. Why was my faith not stronger when it really mattered? Did I even have any faith? What did all this mean? Where was I to go from there?

I began to question why God allowed Paul to be injured and die. I never believed God caused the accident, but I could not understand why He did not prevent the accident from happening. I wondered why God allowed them to close his station. Why did his lieutenant get sick that night? Why did Paul have to be the one who went into the burning building?

As I wrestled with these and many more questions, the thought came to me. God could have intervened. He could have prevented the accident. He could have, but He did not. Just as He could have prevented an accident when a child chases a ball into the street and is killed by an automobile, or a when a drunk driver hits head-on with another driver killing an innocent person. But why should He protect some and not protect others? Why should God protect Paul and not protect everyone? He has placed in motion the natural flow of life. As long as everything moves and performs as designed, the process of nature will take care of everything. When the natural normal flow of life is disturbed, for whatever reason, it brings about serious consequences. Perhaps that is what Dr. Richardson was trying to tell me that night in my office; in short, accidents do happen!

Through all my sorrow and grief, God has always been there as a comfort. I can say without any reservations that God sustained us in our greatest sorrows. Yes, it hurt. It hurt very much. But even in my greatest pain, God gave me strength and comfort. I know without question that if God had ever removed His hand from my life, I could not have made it. I do not believe I could make it now through one single day without the Lord's grace. Thank God I knew Him then! Thank God I know Him now! His grace is sufficient. As the apostle Paul said, we have hope of life beyond this life. Because of that hope, I know that someday I will see Paul again. In fact, I have already sent him a personal message.

Several months following Paul's death, a faithful lady of the church became very ill. She had been transferred to a Jackson hospital for treatment and was very low in ICU. I went in to visit with her shortly before she died. I reminded her of her many years of faithfulness to the church. She had taught Sunday school classes, worked in the church kitchen, led the ladies ministry, and worked in many other areas. I said, "Sis. Lunn, all those years you worked for God and the church, even when many times you didn't feel like doing it, will not be forgotten by the Lord." I continued, "This is what it is all about, when we come to times such as this." I held her hand and told her, "We know it's bad, the doctors are not giving us much hope. But we also know that God can bring you through this and we are praying that He will." Suddenly I made the most unusual request I have ever made. I said, "If this is your time to meet the Lord, after you have settled in a bit, will you look for my boy and tell him that I love him, I miss him, and I will soon join him?" She smiled and replied, "I sure will." I left the hospital that day thinking, *Is that awesome or what? Getting to send a personal message to my son in Heaven.*

Thank God for that eternal hope!

Chapter 14

Fallen Firefighters

Our family was invited to attend the National Fallen Firefighters Memorial Service in October 1990. This is an annual event honoring all firefighters who died in the line of duty the preceding year. The memorial service is conducted on the beautiful campus of the National Fire Academy located in Emmitsburg, Maryland.

We were deeply moved to learn that Paul would be honored along with the other firefighters killed in the line of duty in 1989. This was very special to our family, and we wanted to share this time of recognition and honor for him. Our desire to participate in the memorial service compelled us to make the trip at our own personal expense.

At this same time, we were invited by COPS to attend a special grief seminar to be conducted on Saturday of the memorial service weekend. With his death still less than a year ago, we continued to struggle in our grief and felt the need to attend the grief seminar.

COPS sponsors grief seminars for surviving families of the law enforcement community annually. However, this type of seminar was not yet provided for families of fallen firefighters. The leadership of COPS understood the importance of this program and wanted to extend it to the fire service. The pilot program was conducted at nearby Mount St. Mary's

College on Saturday preceding the Sunday memorial service.

We did not know what to expect when we arrived on campus that cold Saturday morning in Emmitsburg. We had no idea what a grief seminar would involve. Upon our arrival, Suzy Sawyer, the executive director of COPS, warmly greeted us. We were introduced to a number of other surviving families who appeared to have as many questions about the seminar as we did.

A very strange thing happened as I looked into the faces of the other surviving families. It was as if I were looking into a most unusual mirror—a living mirror. I saw the reflection of my own pain and sorrow in their faces. I could see the same sadness that I was experiencing written on their faces; this was an awesome experience. It was not long before I realized we were in a group of very special people.

Survivors had come from across the nation, from different states, different cities, but they all had one thing in common: someone very special in their lives had made the ultimate sacrifice in the line of duty. This was a completely different group than any I had associated with before. It was not a problem with them if I shed a tear when thinking of Paul. It was not necessary to hide my emotions; they required no explanation for my actions—they understood. This alone was therapeutic and proved to be very helpful.

The grief seminar was a tremendous help for each member of our family. We have never regretted the effort we made to attend. In addition to the excellent material covered, we met some truly wonderful people, including Lieutenant Tim and Vickie Taylor, a Virginia firefighter and his wife who is a mental health professional; Dr. Jeffery Mitchell, also a mental health professional; and Chip Theodore, a former firefighter and counselor. These people had a great impact on our lives, and we became very close friends.

The following day the memorial service was conducted on the campus of the National Fire Academy. It was a very emotional experience for each of us. On Sunday morning, we met our escort, Lieutenant Jim Mastin of the Prince William, Virginia, Fire Department. He led us through the day with dignity, professionalism, and genuine sympathy. Jim was a great source of comfort and strength.

The activities began with the morning chapel service, which included special speakers and selected special music. During the chapel service, the name of each firefighter killed in the line of duty in 1989 was read. A huge silver bell sounded after the reading of each name, representing their "last alarm." (I think of this as the "Omega Bell," meaning the "last bell" or "last alarm." Firefighters are called to action by the "alarm," and each of these firefighters being memorialized had heard that "alarm" for the last time.) The service continued with beautiful long-stemmed roses placed in a Maltese cross in memory of each fallen firefighter.

Outside, the weather was wet, cold, and overcast. A large white tent had been erected on the grounds for the outdoor ceremonies. During the ceremony, several speakers delivered words of tribute for the firefighters. A personal message from President George H.W. Bush was read. Each surviving family was presented a United States flag that had flown over the United States Capital Building or the White House.

I had the privilege to meet U.S. Senator Paul Sarbanes of Maryland who expressed his personal sympathy to our family. Senator Sarbanes is a powerful and highly respected voice in the United States Senate and a valuable supporter of the U.S. Fire Services.

We found it rather difficult for us to respond to the honor and recognition given our son that day. It was comforting to know the firefighters who had made the ultimate sacrifice were not forgotten by their nation. For Paul to be honored in such an impressive and dignified memorial service helped restore our family's appreciation for the fire services. It was an honor that we felt had been denied Paul by those who should have given him appropriate recognition.

It disappointed us greatly that a new fire station in Greenville was not named in honor of Paul after city officials said it would be. At the request of the fire chief, the city council voted unanimously to name the new station in Paul's honor. My family attended that particular city council meeting. In fact, the council minutes will substantiate that this measure was passed.

We were also informed that new family units at the Mississippi Firefighters Memorial Burn Center would be named in Paul's honor. Fourteen years have passed since his death, but not one single unit has been named in his memory. If they were not going to follow through with their promises, they should have never made the commitments. Their failure to act on what they promised left our family with the feeling that Paul's death had no meaning. It seemed to us that he died for nothing.

However, at the National Fallen Firefighters Memorial Service, the painful question that echoed within us, "Did he die in vain?" was released. It helped us to see that the nation really did care, that those who had given their lives in the line of duty had not been forgotten. It made us feel very proud of our son for his bravery and for his sacrifice. We left that memorial service with a feeling of pride because our son had been a firefighter!

The following year, I was invited to return as a guest speaker for the grief seminar. To receive an invitation to participate in the memorial was a most humbling experience. I accepted the invitation to speak, and my family joined me for the weekend. In October 1992, I returned as a speaker for the first grief seminar conducted on the campus of the National Fire Academy. This was a very special weekend, because the fire services would embrace the grief seminar and include it in their memorial weekend activities.

In 1992, Congress created the National Fallen Firefighters Foundation. Along with many other programs, the Foundation assumed the responsibilities for conducting the memorial weekend each October. Positive changes were immediately implemented, giving the memorial service greater recognition. The foundation also included a grief seminar as part of the memorial weekend. It has been most gratifying to watch the memorial weekend expand and grow into the observance it is today. Without question, it is one of the most meaningful experiences provided for survivors of fallen firefighters.

Later, I was invited to participate in the development of a training course to be offered to the fire services relating to line-of-duty deaths. After several months of hard work, the training course, *Taking Care of Our Own,* was developed. The Phoenix, Arizona,

Fire Department sponsored the first presentation. The course received immediate acceptance by the fire service leadership and is presently being presented across the nation by the foundation.

Mary Ellis, formerly of the U.S. Fire Administration, is a driving force in the effort to help survivors and fire departments deal with line-of-duty deaths. I first met her in May 1991 while attending the Law Enforcement Memorial Weekend in Washington, D.C. Today, she serves as managing director of the foundation.

It has been my privilege to be involved with the Fallen Firefighters Foundation from the very beginning. My association with the foundation has afforded me the opportunity to share our story with thousands of fire officials around the nation. In each engagement, I focus on helping prevent another family from going through the terrible ordeal our family endured. I consider accomplishing that goal a continuing tribute to our son Paul.

Chapter 15

Unending Journey

There is a definitive difference between the grieving experience and the mourning experience. We approach mourning in a much different way than we do grieving. Mourning may be an individual experience, single and completely alone. It may also be a corporate act by multiple participants, depending upon the circumstances. An entire nation may go into a period of mourning in the death of a hero or national figure. National Day of Mourning proclamations are issued, as well as other significant declarations of expressing national sorrow. On the other hand, a single individual may express mourning by various means—the clothing worn, going into private seclusion, or some other definitive method. Mourning allows public expression of sorrow with honor and dignity by one or by many.

The process of grieving goes much further than the act of mourning. I have found the grieving process requires a tremendous amount of energy. People who grieve usually do not have much energy for anything else. They burn so much physical and emotional energy in the grieving process that they are completely exhausted. It can affect them to the point that they basically have no interest in any other activities. They become literally consumed by the grieving process.

I firmly believe the grieving process is not only unavoidable, but it is also necessary for healing and recovery. It is the natural response of dealing with sorrow and the loss of a loved one. Grieving is an individual thing; no one can grieve for another. There is no set time span for grieving. It takes as long as it takes. For some it may be months. Others may find themselves grieving for years rather than months. The deeper the hurt, the greater the loss; which will require more time for grieving. We have learned the following truism: "The journey of a thousand miles begins with but one single step." The concern is for one to not become locked in at some stage of grief to the point that life has no purpose.

A grieving person needs to find a way to redirect his energy. This is not always easy to do, but it can be done. The sooner one is able to redirect and refocus his energy, the sooner he will find healing. This is not to say that life will return to normal, it never will. The person who has suffered a loss will find a new normal. There will always be emptiness, but one learns to cope with it. In fact, he will find it is possible to refocus his energy toward something positive and do no injustice to the memories of a loved one.

For some time following Paul's death, my wife and I were both wasting away. We suffered a guilt complex—a subconscious feeling that somehow his death was our fault. This is something that will destroy an individual if it is not brought under control. The emotional stress we were under put a strain on our personal relationship. We simply did not have patience with each other as before. We were too consumed with our own grief to be supportive of each other. The biggest problem may have been a subconscious attempt to place blame on each other. I soon learned why statistics reveal that many couples divorce soon after the death of a child. It is a very trying and difficult experience.

In an effort to cope with our grief, we turned to a number of support groups. There are a number of good organizations that offer support to grieving people. Some specialize in supporting parents who loose a child. As good as they are, I was never very comfortable in those groups. I met parents who have been locked in their grief for years that appeared content to remain where they were. Some celebrated their deceased child's birthday as if he were still alive. They spoke of their children in the present tense, never in the past tense. Without criticizing any of these parents, I found that to be too depressing, and it was certainly not what I needed.

One of the most gratifying endeavors for our family has been the Memorial Medical Clinic established in Madras, India, in 1990 in Paul's memory. While serving as international evangelist for the Church of God, Paul Henson had conducted crusades in India where he had seen the great need for such a clinic. He had a strong desire to do something about the suffering he witnessed in Madras, India, especially among the children.

Reverend Henson announced at Paul's funeral that he was going to lead an effort to establish a medical clinic in India and name it in memory of Paul. That touched us very deeply; naturally we wanted to give our support. New Life Church of God in Greenville responded with a large contribution. A number of other churches and individuals also responded with financial support. In February 1990, Brother Henson traveled to Madras, India, and initiated the establishment of the clinic.

The clinic opened in rented facilities with a part-time physician and a full-time nurse. Its mission was to serve the poor people, especially the children of that area of Madras. Many of the people who came to the clinic had never received medical care in their entire lives. Many of the children had never received childhood immunization.

Dr. Jesuvan Sing served as medical director for a number of years providing invaluable service and guidance. Administrative leadership was in the capable hands of the Reverend P.W. Solomon, overseer of the Church of God in India. Under his skillful leadership, property was purchased and a beautiful new building was constructed for the operation of the clinic.

Hundreds of people receive medical treatment in the clinic each week free of charge. They are given medical care, and then they are told about the "Good Physician," the "Great Healer,"—Jesus Christ! Many converts are won each week through this medical ministry.

The clinic has given the opportunity for my family to redirect its grief energy toward something very positive. We are involved in fund-raising through various means for the support of the clinic. For ten years, we sponsored a gospel singing for the Paul Smith Memorial, with the proceeds going to support the clinic. Our greatest support today comes from personal commitments from churches and individuals. The clinic is something the entire family can be involved in, and that is important to each of us.

Another great opportunity for me personally has been my involvement with the National Fallen Firefighters Foundation. My involvement with this organization came about after our family attended the National Fallen Firefighters Memorial in October 1990.

The following year I was invited back as a speaker for a grief seminar.

With the exception of one year, I have participated in the Memorial Service each year since. It has given me an opportunity to share my experience with families who have lost a family member in the line of duty. It gives me personal gratification to be able to help families in their time of grief. If I can help them realize that things will get better in their lives, then I feel my time is well served. This is not altogether unselfish on my part, because each time I am able to help another family, I receive help for myself.

Today, I am honored to travel as a team member in presenting "Taking Care of Our Own." It requires time and effort to share our story in this manner, but I am convinced it is worthy. I do it for two reasons, to honor the memory of our son and prevent another family the nightmare and pain our family experienced.

I understand that others may not have the opportunities I have had. But it is still possible to focus and direct energy toward positive endeavors. There are so many ways a person can accomplish this. Volunteer work is a very good way, and it is always needed in hospitals, nursing homes, and service organizations. Adopting needy people, especially children, during Christmas or an entire family at Thanksgiving. Placing equipment in playgrounds orestablishing a scholarship in the name of your loved one is a great way to memorialize them. A person needs to find the one that is best for them and pursue it.

Almost fourteen years have passed since Paul's death. I have cried many tears during that time. There was a time that I did not think I would ever laugh again. I have had to adjust my life so that I am able to be productive, even if I no longer have Paul's assistance.

There is never a day that passes that I do not think of him at least once and fight back tears as I recall something he did or said. There are still times when I feel that sudden pain in the pit of my stomach, and there are even times when I struggle to breath, but I keep going. I refuse to give up; I have to keep going. I know he would want me to.

The years have taught me one thing—you do not get past the grieving. You learn to cope with it. It is as if I carried a hundred-pound block of ice around my heart for a long time. This block of ice gets smaller with time. One day you will find it has melted to about ten pounds. It may never get any smaller than that. I have learned to live life with a ten-pound block of ice around my heart. That is the hand that fate has dealt me. There is no changing it. I will not wake up from this bad dream and everything will be as it was before. I am on a journey that no one else understands. I keep traveling, moving ahead, and maybe—just maybe—one day I will laugh and look forward to Christmas once again.

Chapter 16

Abandoned

The line-of-duty death of a firefighter is an intensely traumatic experience for the surviving family. Even with strong support from the city and fire departments, the surviving family will face many difficulties in dealing with their untimely loss. Most departments eagerly go above and beyond the call of duty to support a family during the time of tragedy. When a department disconnects from the surviving family, it greatly compounds their already difficult circumstances.

My own personal experience was one of great disappointment right from the beginning of our tragedy. As a parent, I was in a state of shock during the first hours of Paul's injury. At the onset, many things happened so quickly that it was difficult for me to get a grasp of the situation. It was impossible for me to assess logically and intellectually the events and circumstances surrounding Paul's injury. Things were much more confusing for me than it should have been, because I was never given clear, straightforward facts. Fourteen years after the accident, city officials have never told me, "This is what happened, and this is why it happened." City and fire officials immediately displayed a hush-hush attitude toward us. Because of our mental state, we were not able to comprehend it at the time. However, we have later learned facts that may give some insight into why this happened.

We heard the lieutenant's claim that his air pack malfunctioned, causing him to leave Paul and Newton in the building. Such action grossly violated every element of leadership responsibility and displayed a serious flaw of qualification as an officer. One of the strongest and most honored rules of leadership in the fire services is to never leave a burning building until all under a leader's command are out and accounted for. In simple language, the leader should always be the last one out of the building.

Rumors began circulating that the lieutenant's air pack had been checked and found to be in working order. The scuttlebutt around town was that his air pack had not malfunctioned as he claimed. Yet, no one from the city or the fire department shared any straightforward information with me. When I attempted to obtain any facts, I was given double talk and nothing of substance.

I was given a tip to call an investigator who had checked the air pack in question. I made the call and was told by the investigator that indeed the air pack had been checked and it was in perfect working condition. That was distressing information for me to hear. I really did not want to hear that. I could not believe the rumors were true, but his statement confirmed it. Therefore, the only conclusion I could make was that the lieutenant did not have to leave Paul in the burning building. But the fact remains that he did. But, "Why?"

Before our conversation ended, the investigator offered his condolences to our family. He made a remark to the effect that nothing anyone did now could bring Paul back. He said it was truly a sad tragedy. He then told me that should this matter ever come to a trial, he would have to deny giving me that information. I was taken aback by the statement, because it had not crossed my mind to bring a lawsuit against the city. At that time, I never remotely suspected the amount of negligence and cover-up that was involved in the case.

I am absolutely persuaded after giving much consideration to the facts, as I know them, that at the very beginning, the lieutenant made a wrong assessment of the fire. That wrong summation of the fire contributed to a total mismanagement of the situation. I am also convinced that as a department officer, he led Paul and Newton to the second floor to a position directly above the fire. Above the fire was the most dangerous position for them to be in. It is an undisputed fact that he left the two young firefighters in the burning building. In doing so, he compromised leadership responsibility. Witnesses are on record as saying he made no attempt to rescue Paul from the burning building. We also know he allowed several minutes to pass before even acknowledging there was a man down. I recall when the lieutenant came to the hospital on the afternoon of the day Paul was injured, his eyes were bloodshot and he reeked with alcohol. I did not know what to make of it at that time, but today I believe he was a man with a very guilty conscious.

One of the most painful facts for me to deal with is the reality that Paul had been left alone in the fire for several minutes before he was rescued. The doctor in St. Louis told me that if Paul had been moved from the building within two or three minutes, they could have saved his life. The severity of his burns indicated that he remained in the extreme heat and gasses for over seven minutes. He remained in the fire long enough to receive third- and fourth-degree burns to his arms, hands, and his entire face. His lungs and respiratory system also sustained fourth-degree burns.

I was left totally stunned after reaching the shocking conclusion that Paul could have been rescued, if an effort had been initiated. I wanted to know the truth, but I was too emotionally disturbed to pursue it on my own. I found it was possible to want to know the truth, yet at the same time, fear the horror of the truth. The truth can become so painful that one subconsciously develops a guard against it. When Captain Bo Gentry, who pulled Paul from the fire, first offered to talk with me, it was very difficult to initiate the discussion. To me, he is a true hero. I refer to Captain Gentry as an "Angel in Turnouts." If there was ever anyone I wanted to talk with, he was the one, yet it was too painful.

It is very obvious to me now there was an effort by city officials to keep information from us because they feared a lawsuit. We were not thinking about taking legal action. Our only concern was Paul's survival. We were immediately consumed with his injuries and medical treatment. After his death, we plunged into a period of extensive mourning and grieving and thought of nothing else. That is not to say we did not have many questions about what really happened. We had more or less accepted the idea that we would never know the facts and that was the way it would be.

It was only after becoming acquainted with many officials in the fire services that I began to think about taking legal action against the city of Greenville. As time passed, it became clear that there was much more to the total story than we understood. Fire officials I talked with found it difficult to believe we were given so little information and left totally unsupported. The more we shared our story with others, the more strongly we were encouraged to do what was necessary. We were encouraged to force the city of Greenville to accept responsibility in Paul's death. I believed, and I still do, that I owe it to Paul not to allow his death to pass without some kind of action on my part. The clincher came when I was reminded that I had an obligation to the firefighters of the Greenville Fire Department who could be killed because of the same type of negligence. It really was the idea that other firefighters could die unnecessarily that moved me to action.

As time allowed me opportunity to gain more facts concerning the incident, the more convinced I became that I really had no choice in the matter. I must take legal steps to expose a gross negligence on the part of the fire department. An expert who examined the case files concluded there was absolutely no command and control established during the entire incident. The lieutenant said he took command because he was the first officer on the scene. Captain Bob Moore stated that he was the higher-ranking officer on the scene and he took command when he arrived. Unexplainably, he left the scene to obtain a snorkel truck, abdicating his command. Upon arriving at the scene, Assistant Chief Thomas should have taken command and directed the incident, especially the rescue. However, I can find no indication that anyone actually took control and command of the incident. In fact, everyone was doing what they thought was the best thing to do. This created a scene where there was confusion and no combined effort by anyone to plan and direct an attack on the fire. There definitely was no directed rescue effort made by anyone other than Captain Gentry to save Paul.

For these and many other reasons, I came to the uncomfortable decision to initiate legal action against the city of Greenville. Even though nothing of substance has resulted after years of struggling, I am convinced I made the correct choice. As far as I am concerned, it was the only choice.

Several years passed before my wife and I met with Poplarville attorney David R. Smith to discuss the matter. Sitting in on the meeting was attorney Bill Liston of Winona, Mississippi. David accepted the case, knowing full well that it would be a difficult challenge. He filed suit on our behalf against the city of Greenville on September 13, 1993.

My wife and I learned the suit had been filed listening to an evening newscast of a local television station. As soon as the news came out, people began to criticize us for our action. Some said we were hungry for money. Others called it, "blood money." Some even said, "As Christians we should not sue anyone for any reason." The fact that we were being criticized hurt us deeply and caused us additional stress. I could not understand why there was little or no sympathy for us in our loss and only harsh judgment because we took legal action. I can assure anyone we were not out for "blood money." As a matter of fact, we never discussed money with our attorney at any time. It was not about the money. It was about accepting responsibility for Paul's death. It was about correcting a terrible wrong.

There is no way to know just how much time, effort, and money David Smith put into the case. I am confident he left no stones unturned in his quest. From time to time, I would get a phone call or a letter from his office advising us on the case. Occasionally, he would call me into his office for consultation. I was comfortable with David handling the case. It was a long-drawn-out legal process that required a great deal from our attorney. I can say without any reservations that I had the best in David Smith. He had to maneuver past so many legal hurdles it was unbelievable.

At the time of Paul's death, the state of Mississippi had what was called the Sovereign Immunity Law. In laymen's language, it said that the state, county, or city could not be sued. The rationalization behind such a law was that an individual could not sue himself. The state, county, or municipality consists of the people. Individual citizens are the people; therefore, they cannot sue themselves. A municipality could be guilty of gross negligence, even admit their negligence, yet could not be found liable.

Because of the Sovereign Immunity Law, it was necessary for our attorney to make a totally different approach to the case than going for a wrongful death suit. With each attempt to get a trial date, the city attorney of Greenville rebuffed with delay after delay. The defense first argued that we had no grounds for a trial. After repeated attempts, the judge finally allowed the case to go forward. Several years passed before the case was placed on the court docket for trial. The trial date was set for March 8, 1999.

I received a letter from David's office dated August 10, 1998. It said:

Dear Bevon:

We are pleased to inform you that finally we have secured a trial date on the case that we have against the city of Greenville for the wrongful death of your son, Paul. I know that it has been a long time coming, we have had many mountains to climb, but hopefully we are close to bringing this matter to a close. We are enclosing a copy of the Notice of Trial Setting for your review; please give me a call as soon as possible.

With kind regards, we are,
Very truly yours,

David.

Our attorney, David Smith, was suddenly stricken with a fatal illness in December 1998. At his funeral service, his close attorney friend Martin Travis Smith said, "When the judge asked David if he was ready for trial, and David replied, 'Yes, Your Honor, we are ready,' you could believe that he was ready." He always provided his client with the most complete and exhaustive representation possible. I wondered why a man with the ability and legal mind such as he possessed would die so suddenly. I found it very ironic that things connected with Paul followed after his death just as it did in his life. Again, there are some things in life for which there are no answers. I can say without reservations that David Smith was a great attorney and a special friend to our family.

After the death of our attorney, we pondered just where we were and what our next steps should be? An attorney friend of David's in North Mississippi agreed to continue the case. The trial was still scheduled for March 1999. However, once again the Greenville city attorney resorted to tactics to stall, delay, and keep the case from coming to trial. In the following months, there was more maneuvering by the defense, and the case continued to be prolonged.

After months of continual delays, we faced another disappointment when our attorney made the decision to resign from the case. He did make a special effort to secure another law firm to represent us in the case.

At that time, we were discouraged by the continual setbacks. The case was now several years old; in fact, the accident and death had occurred almost 14 years ago. It was a difficult case in the beginning, which became more difficult with time and cold facts. It was clear that many resources would still be required in the case. There were not many law firms eager to invest the effort, especially, with the infamous sovereign immunity clause still hanging over the case.

I discussed the case with an attorney friend from Charleston, Mississippi. At his suggestion, I made contact with a highly respected legal firm in Clarksdale, Mississippi. After reviewing files, discussing the case with our former attorney and an interview with my wife and me, they accepted the case. This firm has rendered very good council, and we are fortunate to have them as our attorneys. From the beginning, we have been reminded of the difficulties in the case. Even though the sovereign immunity law has now been changed in Mississippi, it does not affect Paul's case.

Our present attorney initiated a completely different approach to resolving the matter. They have presented a very fair proposal to the city for consideration. Included in the proposal is the naming of the fire station in Paul's honor as originally promised; the designation of a popular street in his memory; an annual fire department award recognizing the firefighter who contributed the most to training and safety during the year; and a mandatory firefighter safety-training program to be taught within the department by qualified instructors annually. Thus far (2004), the proposal has met with no action by the defendant's council. I personally do not believe the proposal has ever been presented to the mayor or city council for their consideration.

That is Paul's story. That is my heartache.

Afterword

Station Fifty-One

In July 2001, I was speaking to a group of fire chiefs in Los Angeles, California, and I happened to mention that as a child Paul's favorite television program was *Emergency*. Later, Chief Larry Miller, who told me the popular program was filmed in his fire district, approached me and offered to arrange a tour for my family.

When we arrived at the station, the crew warmly greeted us and gave us a tour of the facilities, as well as sharing a bit of its history. A highlight of the visit was when they placed our entire family on the new state-of-the-art fire engine and drove us around the back lot of Universal Studios. We had a first-class tour of the areas that the general public is not allowed to visit.

As we left, I reflected how much Paul loved the television program and none of us ever had the slightest idea we would someday visit that station. It was quite a memorable experience, and I am grateful to Chief Miller for the opportunity.

Greenville Bus Drivers

On Thursday, April 1, 2004, I attended an event sponsored by the State Attorney General's Office at

Mississippi College in Clinton, near Jackson. Students from around the state attended the event, most of whom traveled in school buses. I noticed three buses from the Greenville School District parked with the many other buses. As the day passed, I decided to take a walk and passed by the parked buses from Greenville. Two men were sitting inside one bus talking as I approached. When I spoke to them, I was suddenly jolted with the realization that I knew the man sitting in the driver's seat.

I asked, "Are you Emmanuel Zanders?"

He had a surprised look on his face as he responded, "No, I'm Felix Zanders."

I then asked, "Is he your father?"

Again he replied, "I'm Felix, Felix Zanders."

I continued, "Did you ever work for the fire department?"

He said, "Yes, I still work for the fire department."

Then, I told him, "I'm Paul Smith's father." He literally jumped out of his seat and hugged me like I was a lost brother. It just so happened that the other gentleman was Homer Smith, also a member of the Greenville Fire Department. Homer worked with Paul and knew him very well. He also came out and gave me a big hug.

For several minutes, we sat and talked and shared our stories. It had been 14 years since I last saw them; however, they still talked of Paul as if he were still with them. They told me they talked of Paul every day around the fire station. One said, "There are a lot of young men on the department now who never met Paul, but they know who he was." They hear us older guys talk of Paul continually. They said, Paul Smith was loved by the black firefighters as much as he was loved by the white firefighters. That was because the black firefighters knew Paul loved them too.

After several minutes, the third driver walked up, and Felix asked him, "Tyrone, Do you know who this man is?" He looked at me, but of course he did not know who I was. Felix then asked, "Who was the most loved firefighter by blacks and whites in Greenville?"

Immediately, he responded, "Paul?"

They said, "This is his daddy."

Tyrone hugged me in a big bear hug right there on the parking lot before everybody. I learned that Tyrone is also a member of the fire department and knew Paul as well as the other two did.

Felix looked at me and said, "I told you Paul was loved. You see what I mean?" Ordinarily, I would not have been on that trip. However, I am happy it worked out for me to go, because I would not have missed the opportunity of seeing those guys for anything.

—Bevon Joe Smith